S0-BBM-846

An Industrial Geography of Japan

General editor
PROFESSOR R. O. BUCHANAN
M.A.(N.Z.), B.Sc.(Econ.), Ph.D.(London)
Professor Emeritus, University of London

A. Systematic Studies

GEOGRAPHY AND ECONOMICS
Michael Chisholm, M.A.
AGRICULTURAL GEOGRAPHY
Leslie Symons, B.Sc.(Econ.), Ph.D.
THE WORLD TRADE SYSTEM
SOME ENQUIRIES INTO ITS SPATIAL STRUCTURE
R. J. Johnston, M.A., Ph.D.
LAND REFORM: A WORLD SURVEY
Russell King, B.A., M.Sc., Ph.D.
AGRICULTURE IN THE THIRD WORLD: A SPATIAL ANALYSIS
W. B. Morgan, M.A., Ph.D.

B. Regional Studies

AN ECONOMIC GEOGRAPHY OF EAST AFRICA
A. M. O'Connor, B.A., Ph.D.
AN ECONOMIC GEOGRAPHY OF WEST AFRICA
H. P. White, M.A. & M. B. Gleave, M.A.
YUGOSLAVIA: PATTERNS OF ECONOMIC ACTIVITY
F. E. Ian Hamilton, B.Sc.(Econ.), Ph.D.
RUSSIAN AGRICULTURE: A GEOGRAPHIC SURVEY
Leslie Symons, B.Sc.(Econ.), Ph.D.
RUSSIAN TRANSPORT
(Ed.) *Leslie Symons, B.Sc.(Econ.), Ph.D. & Colin White, B.A.(Cantab.)*
AN HISTORICAL INTRODUCTION TO THE ECONOMIC GEOGRAPHY OF GREAT BRITAIN
Wilfred Smith, M.A.
A GEOGRAPHY OF BRAZILIAN DEVELOPMENT
Janet D. Henshall, M.A., M.Sc., Ph.D. & R. P. Momsen Jr, A.B., M.A., Ph.D.

An Industrial Geography of Japan

EDITED BY
KIYOJI MURATA
Chuo University, Tokyo

ASSOCIATE EDITOR
ISAMU OTA
Toyo University, Tokyo

St. Martin's Press
New York

For information write:
St. Martin's Press Inc., 175 Fifth Avenue, New York, NY 10010
Printed in Great Britain
First published in the United States of America in 1980.

ISBN 0-312-41428-5

Library of Congress Cataloging in Publication Data
Main entry under title:
An Industrial geography of Japan.
Includes index.
1. Japan—Industries—Addresses, essays, lectures. 2. Industries, Location of—Japan—Addresses, essays, lectures. I. Murata, Kiyoji, 1923–
HC462.9.I533 1980 338.0952 80-13404
ISBN 0-312-41428-5

Contents

PART 5 DEVELOPMENT AND DISTRIBUTION OF THE MAIN MANUFACTURING INDUSTRIES – 2

PART 6 INDUSTRIAL LOCATION POLICY AND ENVIRONMENTAL ISSUES

Tables

Figures

Contributors

EDITOR
Kiyoji Murata
Professor, Chuo University, Tokyo

ASSOCIATE EDITOR
Isamu Ota
Professor, Toyo University, Tokyo

Tsutomu Fujimori
Professor, Toyama University, Toyama

Katsutaka Itakura
Professor, Tohoku University, Sendai

Kiei Ito
Professor, Keio University, Tokyo

Masashi Kaneda
Professor, Chuo University, Tokyo

Masayasu Murakami
(Collaborator)
Assistant Professor, Utsunomiya University, Utsunomiya

Hiroshi Naito
Assistant Professor, Ochanomizu University, Tokyo

Atsuhiko Takeuchi
Professor, Nippon Institute of Technology, Miyashiro

Toshifumi Yada
Professor, Hosei University, Tokyo

Shigeru Yamamoto
Assistant Professor, Saitama University, Urawa

Preface

In 1976, when I was a visiting professor in the London School of Economics, Professor Buchanan invited me to write a book on the industrial geography of Japan for this series. Professor Wise and Dr F. E. I. Hamilton encouraged me to accept the invitation and also, along with Professor Buchanan, gave me useful advice about the scope and the plan of the work. I did not, however, commit myself to secure the services of the most appropriate of my Japanese colleagues and to undertake the local editing of the work until I had made sure of the co-operation of Professor Isama Ota, as joint editor, and of Professor Masashi Kaneda and Assistant Professor Shigeru Yamamoto after my return to Japan in the spring of 1977. With them I examined more closely the composition of the book and decided on the allocation of the various parts of the work to the authors most competent to deal with them and on a plan which would ensure a uniform approach and treatment. In the result the book is *not* a symposium of the contributions of the eleven different authors: it is a *book* in which the individual contributions are indistinguishable one from another in treatment and style.

The book is intended mainly for geographers and economists who are interested in Japanese industries, for whom no systematic exposition of the tremendous developments since World War II is available in English. So, in the hope of contributing to a wider and fuller understanding of the processes and results of these developments, set against the background of the pre-war development, we have kept the analyses and explanations general, focusing essentially on organisation and location and eschewing more refined analysis of detail features. In plan the book has six major sections. Parts 1, 2 and 3 examine the formation and the current state of the industrial areas, Parts 4 and 5 the major industries and Part 6, particularly important because Japan started its industrialisation relatively late, the role and the contribution of government.

Translating into English a manuscript written in Japanese is a difficult task for a Japanese and I am grateful for the assistance of Mrs Sachie Hosoki. Even with her help, however, I was conscious that the English version as it left me was Japanese English rather than Englishman's English. Professor Buchanan not only edited that version into its final form, but gave me much general linguistic advice as well. Finally, I must express my appreciation of the work of Mr Hideo Mori and his group, who drew the maps and diagrams for the book.

KIYOJI MURATA

PART ONE
Industrial Development and Characteristics

1

Development of Manufacturing Industries

K. MURATA

During the period when modern industry was already developing in various countries in Western Europe, Japan was still isolated from other countries under the Tokugawa Feudal administration system. The industrial revolution was complete in Britain by about 1835 and in Germany by about 1870. It was not until about 1885 that Japanese private enterprises started to rise but this late start was rapidly made good. With the industrial production index at 100 for the year 1900, the index for Japan for 1937 was 1540 against 350 for the United States of America, 230 for Germany and 170 for Britain.

FROM THE MEIJI RESTORATION TO WORLD WAR I

The Meiji Government (1868–1911), established to replace the feudal system, adopted as its policy 'promotion of industry and high productivity' to establish a capitalistic economic system and to catch up with the levels of European countries, but since private enterprise capital was still short, the Government initiated measures for formation of industrial capital from private commercial funds and the funds accumulated in the agricultural areas, and in addition directly invested government funds and advanced industrialization by state enterprises which introduced advanced technological expertise from foreign countries. In addition to the Army and Navy arsenals, state enterprises in iron and steel, shipbuilding, mining, reeling, spinning, machinery, cement, glass and others were established.

The state enterprises were not wholly successful. They suffered from unfamiliarity with management, friction with foreign engineers and shortage of funds, but they fulfilled their function as pilot plants and were gradually transferred to

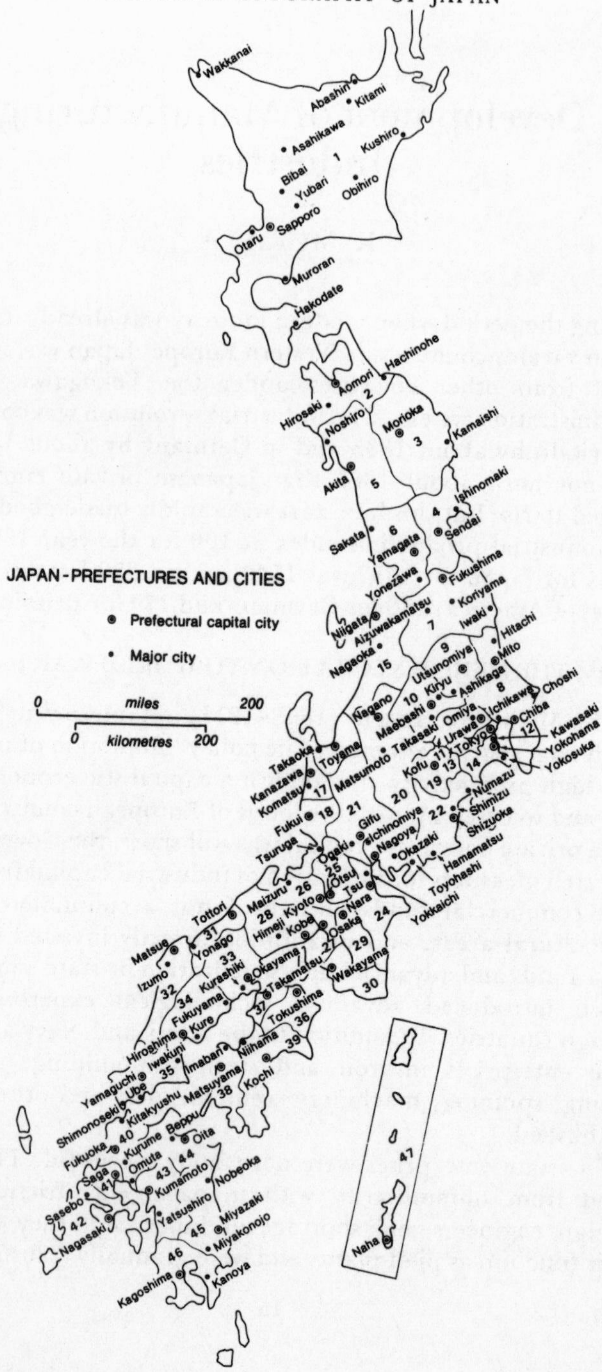

Fig. 1.1 Prefectures and Cities

Reference to Prefectures and Regions

Prefectures		Regions	Prefectures		Regions
1	Hokkaido	Hokkaido	24	Mie-ken	Kinki
2	Aomori-ken	Tohoku	25	Shiga-ken	Kinki
3	Iwate-ken	Tohoku	26	Kyoto-fu	Kinki
4	Miyagi-ken	Tohoku	27	Osaka-fu	Kinki
5	Akita-ken	Tohoku	28	Hyogo-ken	Kinki
6	Yamagata-ken	Tohoku	29	Nara-ken	Kinki
7	Fukushima-ken	Tohoku	30	Wakayama-ken	Kinki
8	Ibaraki-ken	Kanto	31	Tottori-ken	Chugoku
9	Tochigi-ken	Kanto	32	Shimane-ken	Chugoku
10	Gumma-ken	Kanto	33	Okayama-ken	Chugoku
11	Saitama-ken	Kanto	34	Hiroshima-ken	Chugoku
12	Chiba-ken	Kanto	35	Yamaguchi-ken	Chugoku
13	Tokyo-to	Kanto	36	Tokushima-ken	Shikoku
14	Kanagawa-ken	Kanto	37	Kagawa-ken	Shikoku
15	Niigata-ken	Chubu	38	Ehime-ken	Shikoku
16	Toyama-ken	Chubu	39	Kochi-ken	Shikoku
17	Ishikawa-ken	Chubu	40	Fukuoka-ken	Kyushu
18	Fukui-ken	Chubu	41	Saga-ken	Kyushu
19	Yamanashi-ken	Chubu	42	Nagasaki-ken	Kyushu
20	Nagano-ken	Chubu	43	Kumamoto-ken	Kyushu
21	Gifu-ken	Chubu	44	Oita-ken	Kyushu
22	Shizuoka-ken	Chubu	45	Miyazaki-ken	Kyushu
23	Aichi-ken	Chubu	46	Kagoshima-ken	Kyushu
			47	Okinawa-ken	Okinawa

Note: Names of regions are geographical names only

private enterprise from 1880 onwards. Production companies in private enterprise in 1894 numbered 778, of which 54 were cotton-spinning companies, making cotton spinning the leading Japanese manufacturing industry of the time. The spinning industry first used domestic cotton but cheaper cotton imported from India, the United States and elsewhere came to be used more and more, and Japanese original ideas were added to the imported technological know-how. This resulted in good quality production, and the export of cotton products increased gradually after 1920.

On the other hand, the heavy industries, such as shipbuilding, machinery, iron and steel, started their development with the beginning of the 1900's. The Naval arsenals left the hands of foreign engineers, and the building of war-ships was taken over by Japanese engineers. The Nagasaki Shipyard of Mitsubishi Zaibatsu[1], and the Hyogo Shipyard of Kawasaki Zaibatsu, which were transferred from the state, reached international standards, but other shipbuilding enterprises were still at a low level. The production of vehicles increased with the expansion of the railways, and in 1901 the Yahata Iron Works was established under government management and steel production by private capital was started, but development of the machinery industry remained remarkably slow and its activities were largely restricted to copying European products.

DEVELOPMENT BETWEEN THE TWO WORLD WARS

GNP was about doubled in the 25 years after 1880. The contribution of the secondary industries to income increased from 16.3% in 1882 to 21.6% in 1912. In industrial production the spinning industry ranked high, providing 45% of the total output, with food production and the heavy and chemical industries contributing 20% each.

The spinning industry depended upon imported raw cotton and the ratio of the raw material cost, including transport in the production cost, was large because of the transport conditions in those days, but the output per spinning machine was more than twice that of Britain and the United States largely because of the adoption of shift working. The demand for iron and steel increased greatly but Japanese iron and steel technology was still in the infant stage, and therefore two thirds of domestic demand had to be met by imports. In 1913 there were only two blast furnaces of 160 tons capacity in Yahata, and only small private enterprise ones at Wanishi in Hokkaido and Kamaishi in Iwate Prefecture.

[1] *Zaibatsu*, an ancient Japanese term, came to mean a large capitalist organisation or group. Focused on one family, it owned or controlled companies in virtually every sector of the Japanese economy. The Mitsui, for instance, operated in banking, foreign trade, mining, insurance, textiles, sugar, food processing, machinery and other fields. The other main *zaibatsu* were Mitsubishi, Sumitomo and Yasuda. Already large, the zaibatsu grew most rapidly after 1900, especially during World War I, when European war commitments gave Japan great opportunities.

In 1946, dissolution of the zaibatsu by the Allied control, with sales of parent companies' shares and abolition of parent companies' control of individual companies, in effect replaced formal control by informal co-operation, and with the signing of the Japanese peace treaty in 1951 formal regrouping into *zaibatsu*-like organisations recommenced.

In the coal mining industry production was started in the 1880s and grew rapidly, as Table 1 shows. Since, however, the production of coking coal was very limited, imports of coal also increased along with the development of industries. Major coal production areas were Central Hokkaido and Northern Kyushu plus the west end of Honshu, but coal was also produced in the Joban area of Southern Tohuku from small coal seams. The mining machinery, however, was mostly imported and only after 1920 did domestic products become prevalent.

World War I gave an important impetus to the development of Japan's industrial production. Output increased about 3.4 times during 1914–18. The number of factories having 10 or more workers increased to 22,400, which was about 1.8 times, and factory workers to 646,000 persons, which was about two times. The cause of this remarkable development was the expansion of overseas markets owing to the War. At the same time there was gradual progress in the

TABLE 1

Change of Industrial Output in Five Countries

		1900	1913	1919	1929	1936
Coal (million tons)	Britain	229	292	247	262	232
	Germany	109	190	182	163	158
	USA	245	517	545	552	442
	France	33	41	24	54	45
	Japan	8	21	26	34	38
Pig Iron (million tons)	Britain	9.0	10.3	9.2	7.7	7.8
	Germany	7.5	19.3	11.9	13.4	15.3
	USA	13.8	31.0	39.7	43.3	31.5
	France	2.7	5.2	1.3	10.4	6.2
	Japan	0.02	0.2	0.7	1.5	2.9
Steel (million tons)	Britain	4.9	7.7	9.7	9.8	11.9
	Germany	6.4	18.9	15.0	16.2	19.2
	USA	10.2	31.3	45.2	57.3	47.7
	France	1.6	4.7	1.8	9.7	6.7
	Japan	-	0.2	0.8	2.3	5.0
Shipbuilding (thousand tons)	Britain	1,442	1,932	1,620	1,523	1,030
	Germany	205	465	135	249	479
	USA	191	228	3,580	101	163
	France	117	176	33	82	47
	Japan	5	65	612	164	441

Source: H. Arisawa, ed. Gendai Sangyo Koza (Contemporary Industries in Japan), Vol. 1, 1959, p. 165.

development of the heavy and chemical industries. Their share of total industry was 28.8% in 1914 but by 1920 was 36%. The advantage of Japanese industry in overseas markets declined with the ending of the war, but increasing demands in the domestic market favoured continuing development. As Table 1 shows, Japanese industry was developing faster than that of other major industrial countries.

In this period the chemical industries, especially soda, pulp and ammonium sulphate, developed, and the machine industry grew sufficiently to enable spinning machine products to supply the whole domestic demand. In the automobile and aluminium industries, which were then still new industries in the main industrial countries, production had not yet started, and the heavy and chemical industries, not yet well grounded, were generally in an unstable condition. The domestic production of steel goods barely exceeded the amount of imports, and in machine tools imports still exceeded domestic production.

The world-wide depression that started in the autumn of 1929 was a heavy blow to Japanese industries. Many industries were forced to curtail production by 30 to 50% and in consequence drastic wage reduction, personnel cuts and closure of factories occurred successively. The recovery from the depression, however, was faster than in other countries. As Table 2 shows, the level of the pre-depression period had already been restored by 1933.

TABLE 2

Production Index of Main Industrial Countries and Japan

	USA	Britain	Germany	Japan
1929	100.0	100.0	100.0	100.0
1930	83.1	97.9	85.9	94.8
1931	67.8	88.9	67.6	91.6
1932	52.4	88.5	53.3	97.8
1933	62.7	93.5	60.8	113.2
1934	67.8	104.8	79.9	128.7
1935	79.1	112.0	94.0	141.8
1936	93.4	122.7	106.4	151.2
1937	102.7	131.0	117.1	170.8

Source: H. Arisawa, op. cit., p. 221

TABLE 3

Change of Industrial Structure (Per cent of Value)

		1909	1914	1922	1931	1937
Light Industries	Spinning & weaving	50.5	46.4	45.6	37.2	25.8
	Foods	19.1	15.6	16.5	16.2	9.3
	Wood works	2.6	2.1	–	2.8	2.3
	Printing & bookbinding	2.0	2.0	–	3.4	1.7
	Sundries	3.7	3.4	8.8	3.6	3.6
	Total	77.9	69.5	70.9	63.2	42.7
Heavy & Chemical Industries	Ceramics	3.7	2.6	–	2.8	2.5
	Chemicals	11.2	13.2	13.9	15.8	17.8
	Metals	2.2	3.6	–	8.3	21.2
	Machinery	5.3	8.3	13.8	9.6	15.6
	Total	22.4	27.7	27.7	36.5	57.1
	Others	–	1.9	1.4	0.3	0.2

Source: National Institute of Resources, Science and Technology Agency, Kogyo no Kindaika to Ritchi *(Modernization and Location of Manufacturing Industries)*, 1957, p. 47.

Moreover, as Table 3 shows, the output of the heavy and chemical industries exceeded that of light industries in 1937. In 1934, the production of automobiles was stabilised according to government industrial policy, and machine tools, which had been at a low level, also became able to fill domestic demand. This development of the heavy and chemical industries was supported by the advantage in export given by the low yen exchange rate and by the demands by the Sino-Japan Incident (1936). So Japanese industry before World War II had experienced an extremely favourable rate of development, but as Table 1 shows, production of coal, iron and steel in 1936 was so low that it could not stand comparison with that of Britain or the United States.

DEVELOPMENT AFTER WORLD WAR II

Japanese industries suffered greatly from World War II. The production indices of mining and manufacturing in 1946 were only 30 per cent of the pre-war figures (1934–36) and 17 per cent of those of 1941, the pre-war peak. The Japanese economy was paralysed by the shortage of materials and the destruction of production and transport facilities by the air-raids, and the economic chaos was emphasised by the severe occupation policy. A system giving priority to coal, iron and steel as a means of increasing the supply of goods was later replaced by a concentrated production system of supplying funds and materials to enterprises with high production efficiency. Inflation, however, progressed. The government, obliged to tackle this problem by strictly balancing its budget, decided to cut almost all the funds, such as subsidies and special financing, which had been paid for carrying out the industrial policy. These measures reduced inflation, but at the same time effective demand began to fall. So more than 10,000 enterprises were bankrupted between February 1949 and March 1950, and more than 500,000 workers were discharged from employment. This economic stagnation was broken when the Korean War began in June 1950 and the special procurement, 70% of it for metals, machinery and fibres, stimulated industrial production. After the Korean War ended the economic trends suffered some recession, but the stimulation of industrial production by the special procurement had permitted much investment in new equipment and raised productivity by technical modernisation, so that export was expanded. By the later 1950s new industries, such as synthetic chemistry, especially in synthesised fibre and plastics, and electronics began to develop. This consolidated the status of Japan as an industrial country and motivated the following extensive development.

2

Characteristics of Manufacturing Industries

K. MURATA

Manufacturing in Japan has made a striking development since the Meiji Era, and certain characteristics can be seen in the process.

PROTECTIVE POLICY OF THE GOVERNMENT

Since Japan started industrialisation far behind the European countries, state enterprises played the role of pilot plants during the Meiji Era, but concurrently the government also gave protection to private enterprises. Typical examples are the Shipbuilding Promotion Act, 1896, and the Manufacturing Enterprise Act, 1936. The former authorised subsidies for building large ships, and the latter prescribed protective measures for domestic enterprises, such as limitation of production by Ford and GM in Japan, limitation of imports of other American automobiles, higher customs duties on imported cars, and exemption from corporation taxes.

Since national defence expenditure was not to exceed 1% of GNP after World War II, government funds were available for advancement of domestic industries. Private enterprise enjoyed government loans on long term and low interest conditions. Indices of dependence on government funds in the 1950s averaged 40% for electric power, 35% for coal, 23% for metals and fibres and 15% for chemicals, gas and iron and steel. Under the Act for Promotion of Rationalisation of Industries, 1952, rationalisation funds were loaned to 32 different industries which reached a required standard, and other assistance, such as reduction of or exemption from municipal property tax and special depreciation, was also given. Promotion policies for small scale industries provided for granting special rationalisation funds and loans by the governmental financing organs.

DEPENDENCE ON IMPORTED TECHNOLOGY

The leaders in the Meiji Era thought it most important for the modernisation of Japan to reduce the difference in the technical level between Japan and the advanced European countries and the United States. For this reason they strove to improve social conditions and to heighten the level of education as the necessary basis to importing, absorbing and improving on foreign technological expertise. In the early stages engineers, trained workers and machinery were brought from foreign countries, and selected young men were dispatched to Europe and the United States to acquire advanced technological knowledge. In this approach to industrialisation, industrial production in Japan until the end of the Taietzo era (1912–25) was supported by imported technological knowledge and imitated technology.

Japan began to develop her own technological expertise from the beginning of the Showa Era, (1926), but this development was severely hampered while Japan was isolated from other countries during World War II. Particularly, technological competence in passenger car manufacture and thermal power generation was backward, and, further, there was no technological command of high polymer chemistry, electronics, atomic energy and some others. Therefore, liberation of capital was limited and introduction of foreign technological knowledge was actively encouraged to close the dismaying gap in this sphere. Automatic operation and continuous processing became possible by innovation, and large-scale economies were realized. Importing of technological expertise greatly advanced the industrial structure of Japan and enhanced its international competitive power, which formed the basis for the extensive development. Equipment investment, approximately 10% of GNP until the early 1950s, rapidly increased from the later 1950s and had reached 20% by the beginning of the 1960s. The effect of innovation was particularly great in the machinery industry and petrochemistry. The growth of output of manufacturing industry during 1955-61 averaged 2.6 times, but machinery reached 4.5 times and petroleum chemistry 3.1 times. From the early 1960s studies in application of the basic principles of the imported technological knowledge resulted in many advances. In particular original inventions and improvements in iron manufacturing, shipbuilding and electronics were remarkable and promoted the international competitive power of Japanese industry.

LABOUR MARKET

The labour force was supplied mostly from rural areas in the Meiji Era when industrialisation was started. According to Professor M. Umemura's study[1], 91.8% of the industrial labour force in 1875-80 was supplied from rural areas, and even in the period 1910-15 the ratio was 72.5%. This ratio declined from the early part of the Showa Era, but was still 53.4% in 1935. Clearly the industrial labour market depended largely on rural areas, and this remained true even after World War II. According to the research of 1950, the ratio of the male industrial workers from rural areas in factories of more than 500 workers in Kanagawa Prefecture was 48.2%. The industrial workers from rural areas formed employment characteristics peculiar to Japan, such as life-time employment, the wage system based on age and length of service, enterprise, union and so on, but by the 1960s the surge in economic development had brought the number of job offers above the numbers of job hunters, and the employment structure began to change gradually to approach the European type. In consequence the wage level rose gradually until by the early 1970s it was the highest in the world, and the dual structure which existed between major enterprises and minor enterprises was improved. Furthermore, innovation had brought young highly educated workers into playing more important roles than old-type skilled workers and the job-classified wage rate system was gradually added to the traditional wage system based on age and length of service.

DEPENDENCE ON OVERSEAS RESOURCES AND OVERSEAS MARKET

As Table 4 shows, Japan largely depends on imports of major industrial raw materials, and enterprises must have stabilised access to overseas resources in order to maintain

[1] M. Umemura: *Wage-Employment-Agriculture* (in Japanese), 1961, Chap. 8.

industrial production and to enlarge the national economy. This dependence on overseas resources is not new: the state enterprise iron and steel plant established in Yahata in Northern Kyushu in the Meiji Era used Chinese iron ore and coking coal from the beginning, and the cotton industry in the Taisho Era depended entirely on imported cotton. At that time about half the total amount of imports consisted of industrial raw materials.

Given this dependence on overseas resources, it was necessary for manufacturing industries to maximise the value added and to aim at balancing the international payments by increasing exports as well as meeting the domestic demands.

TABLE 4

Ratio of Resources Imports to Consumption in Japan, 1975, Per cent

Coal	76.6
Petroleum	99.7
Iron Ore	99.5
Copper ore	96.8
Rock phosphate	100.0
Timber	55.5
Salt	85.6
Bauxite	100.0
Cotton	100.0
Wool	100.0

Source: Statistics Bureau, Prime Minister's Office, Japan Statistical Yearbook, 1977.

Policies actively encouraging exports were adopted in the same way as industrial production was protected and assisted. The policies were the granting of promotion subsidies for export of designated merchandise, exemption from import duties on industrial raw materials, authorisation of bonded warehouse and bonded factory by law, subsidising of marine transport and so on. Private enterprise, also, endeavoured to limit the rise of wages and to introduce new technological expertise, and took advantage of favourable exchange rates to develop export business further. The export growth rate during 1926-1938 averaged 6.5% per annum which was twice the world average. So trade rivals denounced Japan, alleging commodity dumping and social dumping made possible by the low wage level, and took measures against Japanese merchandise such as raising import duties and restricting imports. The chief export items in 1907 were raw silk (26.9%), cotton cloth (10.8%) and silk cloth (7.3%), and the export of cotton cloth increased rapidly after 1910.

The outbreak of World War I drastically reduced the exports of the participating countries and Japan expanded her share in Asian markets and in addition developed markets in Australia, South America, and Africa, which greatly increased the amount of export. The trade balance continued in the red during the chronic depression period of the 1920s, but exports gradually increased after 1930. In particular the exports of cotton cloth passed those of Britain and gave Japan top position in the world. From the later 1930s, however, the Japanese economy was under the war-time system, and industrial production and international trade were placed under the control of the Government. Then trade was mostly with Asian Yen Bloc countries, and Japan came to depend on Asian countries for most of her industrial raw materials.

From 1955 the export of industrial products became active, following the periods of stagnation and revival after World War II, and among the export items heavy and chemical industrial products took the top position, reflecting the advancement of the industrial structure. The share of the heavy and chemical products increased from 38.1% in 1955 to 67.9% in 1968. The main export items were steel, ships, cars, radios, television receivers, cameras (Table 5), and the export markets were North America, Asia and Europe in that order: these three took 80% of total exports.

TABLE 5

Ratio of Exports to Industrial Production in Japan, 1975, Per cent

Synthetic fibre fabrics	71.3
Crude steel	33.6
Machine-tools	26.7
Television receivers	46.6
Cameras	70.0
Passenger cars	40.7
Ships	85.9
Watches & clocks	59.3
Urea	69.7
Tyres & tubes	58.2

Source: Statistics Bureau, Prime Minister's Office, Japan Statistical Yearbook, 1977.

3

Position of Japanese Industry

M. KANEDA

Japanese industry suffered a destructive blow from World War II, but the special procurement boom at a turning point of the Korean War in 1950 gave it another chance to develop. Mining and manufacturing production in 1951 had already regained the level of 1934–36. Thereafter, exports increased with the enlargement of the world economy and the rapid expansion of the scale of industry to meet the increase of demand for consumption resulting from the increase of national income. In addition, the ratio of the employees in manufacturing industry to the total employed population increased from 21.2% in 1940 to 24.2% in 1965 and further to 26.0% in 1970, but some recession in 1975 reduced the figure to 24.9%. The contribution of manufacturing industry to the net national production was 27.8% on average for 1973-75. These levels compare well with those of other advanced industrial countries. Table 6 shows the comparative numerical values in advanced industrial countries of the ratio of the employees of manufacturing industry to the total employed population, and Table 7 shows the contribution of mining and manufacturing to the gross national product. In the former, West Germany is somewhat higher than other countries, but Japan has already

TABLE 6

Industrial Workers in Employed Population (%)

Name of State	Ratio of Industrial Workers
Japan (1975)	24.9
USA (1974)	24.5
Britain (1974)	34.4
W. Germany (1974)	39.4
France (1974)	27.9

Source: ILO, Yearbook of Labour Statistics, 1975.

overtaken the 24.5% of the United States. The latter shows that Japan exceeded the figures of the United States and Britain.

TABLE 7

Contribution Share of Mining & Manufacturing Industries in GNP (%)

Name of State	Contribution Share
Japan (1975)	27.2
USA (1973)	26.8
Britain (1971)	26.8
W. Germany 1975[1]	42.6
France 1974[1]	35.8

Source: U. N. Monthly Bulletin of Statistics [1]Including electricity, gas, and water supply

On the other hand, in the process of economic growth the increase in the growth rate of the heavy and chemical industries over that of the light industries occurred simultaneously with the development of the industrial structure, as pointed out by W. Hoffman. The ratio of workers in the heavy and chemical industries increased rapidly from 35.5% in 1935 to 56.2% in World War II. The ratio decreased temporarily after the war but rose again to 50.3% in 1973. Table 8, comparing four advanced countries, shows West Germany as leading other countries, with Britain second and Japan third in the ratio of workers in heavy and chemical industries. A specific feature is the fact that in any country the relative importance of the machinery industry is high.

TABLE 8

Ratio of Heavy and Chemical Industries in Advanced Countries by Ratio of Workers (%)

Industrial Department	Japan (1974)	USA (1973)	UK (1974)	W. Germany (1975)
Heavy/Chemical Industry	50.5	49.7	57.4	65.6
Metals	14.1	14.1	13.8	17.2
Machinery	31.9	30.7	37.6	40.0
Chemicals	4.5	5.0	6.0	8.4
Light Industries	49.5	50.3	42.6	34.4
Total	100.0	100.0	100.0	100.0

Sources: Japan, MITI, Census of Manufacturers, 1974. USA, Statistical Abstract of the United States, 1975. W. Germany, Statistisches Jahrbuch für die Bundesrepublik Deutschland, 1976.

By scale of factory in three advanced countries the ratio of workers employed by factories of 1–99 workers is 53.0% in Japan, 24.8% in USA and 19.6% in West Germany, which indicates considerable differences. The weight of employment in factories of 100–499 workers is high in West Germany and of 500–999 workers is high in the United States.

Table 8 summarises comparatively the position of Japanese industry but some further characteristics may be noted.

1. The machinery industry among the heavy and chemical industries made rapid growth throughout the extensive development period. In 1974 it employed 31.9% of the total manufacturing workers, provided 30.3% of total shipments and 32.5% of total value added. Exports, too, in 1974 reached 27,119 million dollars, which ranked it third in the world, although well below the 40,900 million dollars of the United States and the 40,277 million dollars of West Germany. In particular, exports of cars, ships, radio sets, television sets, cameras, far exceeded those of other foreign countries.

2. Japan is well known for the importance of its small-sized factories. As Table 9 shows, the ratio of 1–99 workers scale factories decreased between 1955 and 1957, but they still account for 97.7% of the total number of establishments, 53.0% of the total number of workers and 35.0% of the total shipments. These are high percentages.

TABLE 9

Classification of Manufacturing Industries according to number of persons engaged (%)

Scale of Establishment	Number of Establishments		Persons Engaged		Shipments	
	1955	1973	1955	1973	1955	1973
1–99	98.6	97.7	60.7	53.0	39.2	35.0
100–299	1.0	1.7	12.9	16.0	16.9	17.3
300–999	0.3	0.5	11.8	14.8	20.4	21.1
1000 or more	0.1	0.1	14.6	16.2	23.5	26.6
Total	100.0	100.0	100.0	100.0	100.0	100.0

Source: Census of Manufacturers, 1955, 1973

In Japan companies of less than one hundred million yen capital are classified as minor business corporations under the provisions of Minor Business Basic Law, as amended in October 1973. On this classification minor business corporations total 93.7% of the number of establishments, employ 51.0% of the number of workers and provide 33.8% of the amount of shipments. This high importance of minor enterprises is peculiar to Japanese industry, but most of them have close relationships with large enterprises as their subcontractors. There are differences between minor enterprises and large enterprises in wage rates, productivity, capital-labour ratio, etc. For instance, the differences in 1973 between enterprises with more than 1,000 workers and those in the minimum scale of 20–29 workers were as follows: Wage per capita — 100.0:63.1, productivity — 100.0:48.5, capital-labour ratio — 100.0:33.1.

3. The technological level of Japan is still backward in the fields of space industry and atomic energy industry, but the technical ability for the creation of various industrial products will stand comparison with that of any other country. Most of the technological aid was introduced from the United States and Europe, and it has been said that Japanese technological expertise is better at improvements or applications than in basic matters. There were 2,465 imports of technological aids from 1949 to 1966, 1,442 in machinery, 447 in chemicals (mainly petro-chemicals) and 182 in metals, and this imported command of technology stimulated new industrial development. For instance, plastics, man-made fibres and other products, produced by the development of organic synthetic chemistry or macro-molecular technology, provided the basis for the growth of a huge industrial belt in the coastal region.

4. The rapid development of industry also brought about serious industrial pollution. The pollution-related diseases, such as the so-called Minamata disease, the second Minamata disease, Yokkaichi asthma and others, have spread Japan's reputation as a representative pollution-stricken country no less than as a representative industrial country.

Although the industry of Japan developed rapidly after World War II, its fragile nature was exposed by the oil panic that struck suddenly in 1973. Japanese industry had to face a very difficult situation through the restriction of imported raw materials, industrialisation of developing countries, and, further, industrial, environmental and pollution problems, which grew more and more serious.

4

Regional Structure of Manufacturing Industries

M. KANEDA

OLD INDUSTRIAL REGIONS AND NEW INDUSTRIAL REGIONS

The Japanese manufacturing industry has about seven hundred thousand establishments, employing approximately 11,500,000 workers to produce annual shipments of 127.3 billion yen. The geographical distribution of these production

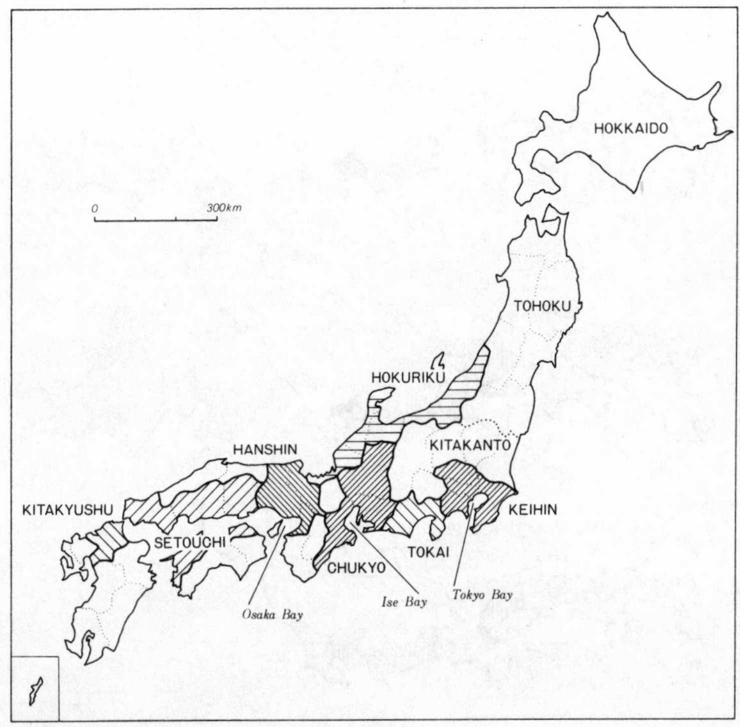

Fig. 1.2 Share of shipments by prefecture

activities may be divided into concentrated areas and straggling areas. Figure 1.3 shows the shipment shares of Prefectures in the total shipments of the country for three years, 1938, 1955 and 1974. So this evolution of industrial distribution covers almost 40 years. In 1938 there were already superior industrial areas, now called the old industrial regions. In addition new industrial regions were born in the development process of industrial agglomeration between

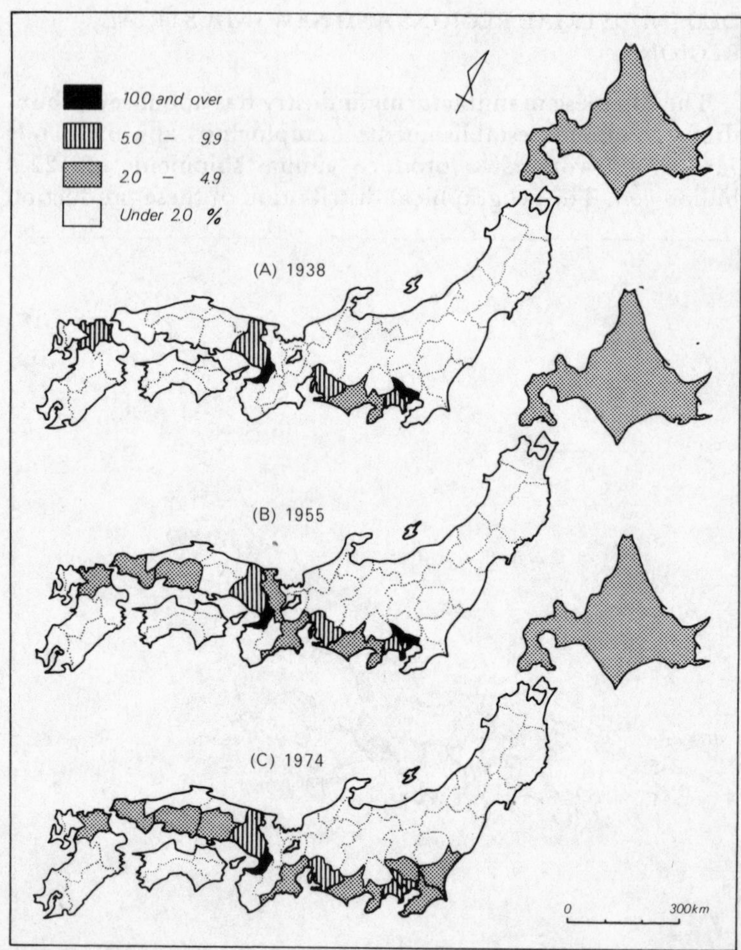

Fig. 1.3 Industrial regions

1955 and 1974. These two types of industrial regions will now be discussed.

1. The old industrial regions or the four major industrial areas. According to Figure 1.3, the areas that provided more than 10% each of the total shipments of the country were Osaka (16.44%), the top area, and Tokyo (16.11%); 5 to 9.9% of shipments were made by the four Prefectures, Hyogo (9.00%), Fukuoka (8.61%), Kanagawa (8.53%) and Aichi (7.42%); 2% to 4.9% of shipments were made by two Prefectures, Hokkaido (2.35%) and Shizuoka (2.32%); all other Prefectures indicated less than 2%. Clearly, the industrial distribution at that time was extremely unbalanced. Areas of Keihin (Tokyo and Kanagawa), Hanshin (Osaka and Hyogo), Northern Kyushu (Fukuoka), Chukyo (Aichi), the four major industrial areas, held outstanding positions.

TABLE 10

Change of Regional Share of Industrial Shipment (100 million yen)

A. Old Industrial Areas

	Keihin	Hanshin	Chukyo	Northern Kyushu	Total	Japan
1955	14,580	13,633	7,308	3,283	38,804	67,720
Per cent	(21.5)	(20.1)	(10.8)	(4.9)	(57.3)	(100.0)
1974	237,271	207,171	140,775	34,969	620,185	1,273,080
Per cent	(18.6)	(16.3)	(11.1)	(2.7)	(48.7)	(100.0)

Source: Census of Manufacturers

B. New Industrial Areas

	Northern Kanto	Keiyo	Tokai	Setouchi	Total	Japan
1955	3,467	872	2,683	4,079	11,101	67,720
Per cent	(5.1)	(1.3)	(4.0)	(6.0)	(16.4)	(100.0)
1974	128,540	51,289	53,513	98,021	331,363	1,273,080
Per cent	(10.1)	(4.0)	(4.2)	(7.7)	(26.0)	(100.0)

Source: Census of Manufacturers

Northern Kanto includes Saitama, Tochigi, and Gumma Prefectures. Tokyo Metropolitan Area, as mentioned in and after Chapter 2, means an area where a part of Keihin in Table 10A above and Northern Kanto and Keiyo in Table 10B above are joined. For other areas refer to the text.

2. *New industrial areas.* During World War II manufacturing industry experienced expansion and dispersal by government control and, further, severe damage by air raids, but circumstances changed after the war. When industrial shipments in 1955 are viewed, one finds new tendencies (Fig. 1.3B). The first thing to notice is that among the old industrial regions the share of Northern Kyushu industrial region had been reduced to 4.78%. The second is that the regions adjacent to the old industrial regions, such as the Setouchi coastal belt of Hiroshima and Yamaguchi Prefectures, and Kyoto and Mie Prefectures had improved their position. This tendency was intensified by the extensive development which started from the beginning of the 1960s, as shown in Figure 1.3C. Among these regions the following are representative.

(i) The outer region of Keihin industrial area. By 1974 the relative importance of Tokyo had declined to 9.1% and the relative importance of regions adjacent to the Keihin area, such as Saitama, Ibaraki, Chiba (Keiyo), increased. This expansion into outer regions extended to Prefectures in northern Kanto, such as Gumma, Tochigi.

(ii) Tokai industrial region. Industrial production in Shizuoka was 3.94% in 1955, but it registered a steady growth until 1974, when its share was 4.2%. Presumably Shizuoka's location between Keihin and Chukyo acted advantageously.

(iii) Setouchi industrial region. Okayama, Hiroshima and Yamaguchi, which face the Seto Inland Sea, formed the industrial region on the basis of the various advantages of this sea.

3. *Other industrial areas:* In northern Japan, various kinds of industrial activities are seen in the cities of Hokkaido, Muroran, Kushiro, Tomakomai, Hakodate, Sapporo, Otaru. In the Tohuku region new industrial agglomerations are being formed in New Industrial Cities, such as Hachinohe, Akita Bay, Sendai Bay, Joban-Koriyama, and in inland areas of Fukushima and Yamagata. Furthermore, agglomeration of indigenous industries is seen in the Suwa basin of Nagano and Toyama, Takaoka, Ishikawa and Fukui cities in the Hokuriku region. In southwestern Japan, industries are gradually advancing to the Pacific Coastal Belt of Shikoku Island and the Japan Sea coastal Belt and some Prefectures in middle and

northern Kyushu.

The industrial regions of Japan, focussed on the old industrial regions (Table 10A) and the new industrial regions (Table 10B), account for approximately 75% of the total production. The old industrial regions and the new industrial regions among the above-mentioned will be analysed from the viewpoint of locational characteristics.

Firstly, all the major industrial areas are located in the Pacific Coast Belt, and Northern Kyushu and Setouchi may also be regarded as belonging to the Pacific Coastal Belt. Furthermore, the four long-established major industrial areas are without exception located behind representative ports. Since Japan lives by processing large quantities of raw materials from overseas and by exporting the products, location in port areas was an important requirement. At the same time, however, since big cities developed in the hinterland of these ports, the port-orientation enables raw material operations to cater conveniently for the large consuming population also. In addition, location adjacent to big cities makes it possible to obtain various kinds of labour and enjoy various kinds of external economies. Secondly, these industrial areas are distributed westwards from Kanto Region. In Tohuku and Hokkaido Regions industrial agglomeration is still weak; industries are at an early stage of development. In these areas industrial development was delayed because of natural conditions, such as relief of the land, weather (snow accumulation in winter), and social and economic conditions, such as undeveloped traffic systems and lack of external economies, but the industrial environment should be improved by the completion of the Tohuku Super-express Railway, Tohuku High Way and Seikan Tunnel (a sub-marine tunnel which couples Aomori and Hokkaido), which are under construction. Thirdly, there is a problem of locational relevancy between the old industrial regions and the new industrial regions. More detail on the old industrial regions is given in Section 3, (p. 93), but these regions, dating from the Meiji Era, have outgrown the advantages of large-scale economies attributable to the innovations of World War II and the contact advantages of regional agglomeration. For instance, the difficulty of expanding industrial land and the external diseconomies concerning port facilities, roads and traffic and industrial pollution have created economic and social problems. The intention to overcome these problems gave an impulse and a timing to the forming of new industrial regions. The Keihin industrial region expanded to outer areas and industries diffused to such northern Kanto prefectures as Ibaraki, Gumma, and Tochigi. On the other hand a new industrial area was formed in the coastal belt of Chiba Prefecture by reclamation. New industrial regions, such as Tokai and Setouchi, are formed in the gaps between the four major industrial areas and their shipments are increasing year by year. The shares of the shipments of the above-mentioned industrial regions indicate the following characteristics:

1. The four major industrial areas in 1974 provided 48.7% of the total shipments of the country, equivalent to 1.87 times the share of the new industrial regions, which was 26.0%, so that the relative importance of these four major industrial areas was still large. The order of individual contribution of the four major industrial areas is Keihin, Hanshin, Chukyo and Northern Kyushu.

2. Among the shipment ratios of the new four industrial regions North Kanto's is as large as 10.1%, which is close to the 11.1% of Chukyo, and the industrial share of the Tokyo Metropolitan Area is 26.8% (32.7% if Tochigi and Gumma are included). Clearly the Tokyo Metropolitan Area has become the area of the largest industrial agglomeration.

3. Between 1955 and 1974 the share of the four major industrial areas decreased by 8.6%, and the advance of the new industrial regions was extremely large. The figures show that Chukyo achieved a very slight increase, 0.3%, but all other major industrial areas showed decrease. On the other hand, among the new industrial regions Northern Kanto's share almost doubled and Keiyo's trebled.

The expansion of productive capacity in the new industrial regions contributed greatly to the extensive development that started in the 1960s. How such industrial regions were created is of importance to students of the regional structure of Japanese industry. The persons responsible for constructing factories and promoting productive activities were entrepreneurs, managers of private capital, who aimed at maximisation of profits. While, however, a tremendous amount of investment was required to provide the infrastructure, most of the cost of large scale reclamation and of preparation of industrial estates was defrayed by public investment in accordance with the regional development policy. The amount of public investment from 1960 to 1969 totalled about 34 billion yen, of which roads, ports and harbours, railways, telegraphic communication, which are investment related industries, received 54.8%. Internalisation of the external economies generated by these infrastructure developments enhanced the efficiency of private capital of enterprises in the new industrial regions.

Secondly, the role played by the wide-ranging innovation after World War II must be mentioned. For instance, the development of civil engineering techniques of reclamation of shoaling beaches and construction of excavated ports made seaside industrial areas possible. Further, the development of engineering and chemical techniques applied to iron ore realised enlargement of production equipment and invited the appearance of the typical Japanese industrial complex. Thirdly, most former fishing villages and farming villages accepted such regional reorganisation, despite many problems, many areas welcoming preparation of new industrial estates, though in some the original plan had to be reduced or abandoned through the opposition of the residents. Fourthly, local governments adopted positive inducement policies. It was expected that large scale industrial development would have a great economic impact on the local area concerned, major effects being financial, employment, income to tertiary industries and so on. Lastly, demand supported the productive effort generated by the large-scale industrial development. With the need for revival after World War II and following the special procurement demand to meet the Korean War came increased external demand for exports to the United States and South-East Asian countries, and the increased internal demand to satisfy rising standards of consumption.

This formation of new industrial regions broke the bottleneck of the old four major industrial areas and also realised the advancement of the people's consumption level through the widespread and vast increase of production.

REGIONAL STRUCTURE WITH REFERENCE TO INDUSTRIAL CLASSIFICATION

An important factor in this extensive development was the development of heavy and chemical industries. The characteristics of Japanese industrial areas from the viewpoint of industrial classification are as follows.

From 1955 to 1974 (Table 11), the share of heavy and chemical industry increased from 44.6% to 62.5% and the amount of shipments increased by 1.40 times. Mechanical engineering registered an especially remarkable increase: its shipments increased 2.06 times. Then the metallic industry and chemical industry follow, but in the chemical industry the relative ratios in the number both of establishments and of employees decreased. So mechanical engineering was the leading sector in the extensive development.

TABLE 11

Change of Type of Industries (%)

Type of Industry	Number of Establishments		Number of Employees		Amount of Shipment	
	1955	1974	1955	1974	1955	1974
Total	100.0	100.0	100.0	100.0	100.0	100.0
Metals	7.7	13.8	11.7	14.1	17.0	19.2
Machinery	8.7	16.5	18.5	31.9	14.7	30.3
Chemicals	2.2	0.9	7.2	4.5	12.9	13.0
Heavy & Chemical	18.6	31.2	37.4	50.5	44.6	62.5
Food	22.0	12.3	12.5	10.0	17.9	10.3
Textiles	20.6	21.5	21.8	13.2	17.5	6.6
Ceramics	5.8	4.6	5.3	5.0	3.4	3.8
Others	33.0	30.4	23.0	21.3	16.6	16.8
Light Industry	81.4	68.8	62.6	49.5	55.4	37.5

Source: Census of Manufacturers, 1955, 1974

The amounts of industrial products shipped in 1974 as classified by the eight industrial regions mentioned above are indicated in Table 12, which shows considerable differences in industrial structure among the industrial regions.

For the whole country, heavy and chemical industry provided 62.5% in 1974, with two of the eight industrial regions, Northern Kyushu and Tokai, below the average and the other six above it. Particularly high are the 76.5% of Keiyo, 72.8% of Setouchi, and 70.0% of Keihin. Keiyo and Setouchi owe their very high percentages to being new industrial regions, where also agglomeration of pre-existing light industries had been weak. On the other hand Northern Kanto and Tokai are still relatively weak in heavy industry, since they had had agglomeration of various kinds of light industries, especially fibres. Among the existing industrial regions, Northern Kyushu has a comparatively high share in iron and steel, but over the whole of heavy and chemical industries is smaller than other regions, since the agglomeration of metallic and mechanical departments - other components of the heavy and chemical industries - is small. In Keihin, where the share of heavy and chemical industries is highest, the engineering industry is outstanding. Table 13 shows the 'location quotient', computed from Tables 11 and 12.[1]

According to this table Setouchi, Northern Kyushu, and Keiyo show high shares in metallic industry and Keihin, Chukyo, and Northern Kanto in the machinery industry. In the chemical industry Keiyo is outstanding, with 2.49, followed by Keihin.

In the above heavy and chemical industries Northern Kyushu and Tokai have a quotient of less than 1 and all other regions are more specialised than the average of the whole country. Among the light industries there is regional specialisation in the food industry in Northern Kyushu, Keiyo, and Tokai, in textiles in Hanshin and Chukyo and in other types in Tokai and Northern Kyushu.

[1] Location quotient is obtained by the formula

$$\frac{Ai}{At} \bigg/ \frac{Ni}{Nt}$$

where shipment of a certain industry in a certain region is represented by Ai, total industrial shipment by At, national shipment of the same industry by Ni, and total national industrial shipment by Nt. (See Florence, P.S., *Investment, Location and Size of Plant*, Cambridge University Press, 1948.)

TABLE 12

Share of Shipment of Industrial Product by Major Industrial Area (1974) (%)

Industrial Region	Heavy and Chemical Industries				Light Industries				
	Metals	Machinery	Chemical	Total	Food	Textile	Others	Total	Grand Total
Keihin	13.6	42.8	13.6	70.0	8.3	1.8	19.9	30.0	100.0
Hanshin	27.9	27.2	11.1	66.2	9.4	6.7	17.7	33.8	100.0
Chukyo	16.0	40.2	9.6	65.8	7.4	9.7	17.1	34.2	100.0
Northern Kyushu	31.9	15.0	10.5	57.4	14.5	2.4	25.7	42.5	100.0
Northern Kanto	20.4	37.0	7.1	64.5	9.2	5.0	21.3	35.5	100.0
Keiyo	31.8	12.3	32.4	76.5	10.7	1.1	11.7	23.5	100.0
Tokai	11.2	34.8	10.5	56.5	10.6	4.7	28.2	43.5	100.0
Setouchi	23.8	23.1	25.9	72.8	7.4	5.3	14.5	27.5	100.0

Source: Census of Manufacturers, 1974

Industries in which industrial specialisation is advanced in areas other than the eight major industrial regions, particularly those of more than 2.0 locational quotient (1974), are the lumber and wood and the food and tobacco industries of Tohuku, the petroleum and local products, non-ferrous metals, textile, pulp and paper of Shikoku, and the food, tobacco and lumber and wood products industries of Kyushu.

TABLE 13

Locational Quotient of Major Industrial Regions

Region	Heavy and Chemical Industries				Light Industries			
	Metals	Machinery	Chemicals	Total	Food	Textile	Others	Total
Keihin	0.71	4.41	1.05	1.12	0.81	0.27	0.97	0.80
Hanshin	1.45	0.90	0.85	1.06	0.91	1.02	0.86	0.90
Chukyo	0.83	1.33	0.74	1.05	0.72	1.47	0.83	0.91
Northern Kyushu	1.66	0.50	0.81	0.92	1.41	0.36	1.25	1.13
Northern Kanto	1.06	1.22	0.55	1.03	0.89	0.76	1.03	0.95
Keiyo	1.66	0.41	2.49	1.22	1.04	0.17	0.57	0.63
Tokai	0.58	1.15	0.81	0.90	1.03	0.71	1.37	1.16
Setouchi	1.24	0.76	1.99	1.16	0.72	0.80	0.70	0.73

Source: Census of Manufacturers, 1974 (computed from Tables 11 and 12)

LABOUR PRODUCTIVITY AND WAGE LEVEL AS CLASSIFIED BY REGION

In this section labour productivity and wage levels will be discussed and their regional characteristics analysed to observe the regional structure of Japanese industry, although these topics are unusual in the field of geography. Labour productivity is obtained from the value added per employee of a manufacturing industry, and regional differences in labour productivity depend to a considerable extent on the type of industry. At the same time wage level has a close relationship with labour productivity. Regional characteristics in labour productivity and wage level (total payment/number of employees) are as follows.

The national average of labour productivity was 4.04 million yen, and 15 of the 47 prefectures exceeded the average. Of these 15, Tokyo, Kanagawa, Chiba and Saitama, all of them in Keihin industrial region, occupied the first four places. In Northern Kanto, Ibaraki's high numerical value is considered to be the result of the constitution of Kashima Coastal Region, which was designated as a Special Area for Industrial Consolidation. In Hokuriku region Ţoyama is above the average and the highest on the Japan Sea Coastal Belt, all other prefectures in that belt being below the average. The areas above average are the Tokai and Chukyo regions, which include Aichi Prefecture and Shiga Prefecture. The Hanshin region, which includes Osaka, Hyogo and Wakayama Prefectures, follows. In the Setouchi Industrial Region, Yamaguchi and Ehime Prefectures exceeded the average. In Kyushu, Fukuoka Prefecture, which includes Northern Kyushu industrial region, slightly exceeds the average, but other prefectures are low. In wage level 10 prefectures are above the national average of 1,560,000 yen. The prefectures where labour productivity is above the average but the wage level is below it are Ibaraki, Toyama, Mie, Shiga, and Wakayama Prefectures. On the other hand, the prefectures where the wage level is above the average while the labour productivity is below it are Kyoto and Hiroshima Prefectures.

PART TWO
The Three Major Industrial Regions

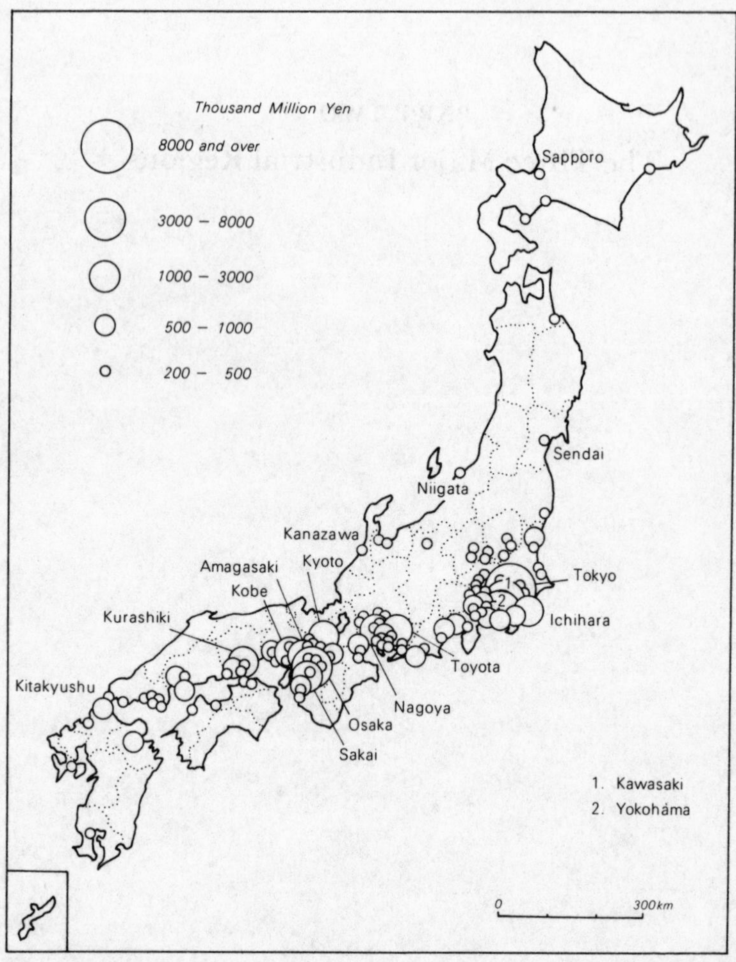

Fig. 2.1 Distribution of main industrial cities by shipment, 1975

1

The Keihin Region

K. ITAKURA AND A. TAKEUCHI

OUTLINE OF THE AREA

The Keihin industrial region, centering on Metropolitan Tokyo, includes Metropolitan Tokyo and Yokohama in a belt along Tokyo Bay, and now continues over four prefectures, Tokyo, Kanagawa, Saitama and Chiba, forming the largest industrial region in Japan. In this area huge chemical plant groups are conspicuous along the Tokyo Bay coastal area, but development of industries inland is also remarkable. In the 1920s the 'Keihin region' included only two prefectures, Tokyo and Kanagawa, but in the 1950s Saitama Prefecture was included and in the later 1960s Chiba Prefecture (Keiyo) was added. The expanded Keihin region is also called Southern Kanto from its position, and its scope includes the old region and the new region mentioned in Part 1. Development of factories in Tochigi, Ibaraki and Gumma Prefectures in Northern Kanto, which surround the expanded Keihin region (Southern Kanto) also became active from the later 1960s. In output, however, Northern Kanto is still extremely small as compared with Southern Kanto.

POSITION IN THE WHOLE COUNTRY

The number of industrial workers in Keihin region in 1974 was 2,685,000, which was 23.4% of that of the whole country; the value of industrial shipments was 26.8%; and the value added was 27.7%. This difference in nationwide ratio between the number of workers and the value of industrial shipments shows the high productivity of the industries in the Keihin Region.

TABLE 14

Change of Workers' Numbers in Keihin and Kinki Industrial Regions (in thousands)

	1950	1955	1960	1965	1970	1974
Japan	3861 (100.0)	5519 (100.0)	8169 (100.0)	9921 (100.0)	11680 (100.0)	11503 (100.0)
Keihin	759 (19.7)	1208 (21.9)	2036 (24.9)	2569 (25.9)	2942 (25.2)	2685 (23.3)
Kinki	867 (22.5)	1214 (22.0)	1823 (22.2)	2092 (21.1)	2361 (20.1)	2210 (19.2)

Source: MITI, Census of Manufacturers. Keihin = Tokyo, Kanagawa, Saitama, and Chiba. Kinki = Osaka, Kyoto, Hyogo, Shiga, and Nara.

Keihin's percentage of the national output reached a peak in 1970 and then gradually decreased, but absolute figures remain very high both in the value of shipments and in the number of workers. Keihin region progressively expanded industrial agglomeration in the extensive development period of the Japanese economy. As Table 14 shows, it was during the five years from 1955 to 1960 that the increase in the number of workers, amounting to some 828,000, was most remarkable. The rate of increase gradually slackened thereafter and has become an absolute decrease since 1970. The economic recession after the oil panic in 1973 is one of the major factors in this decrease. For the Keihin region the golden age in industrial development was in the early stage of the rapid growth period of Japan, when almost 70% of the increase in industrial workers in Japan was absorbed by the three major metropolitan areas of Tokyo, Nagoya and Osaka, 45% of it by Keihin region alone. The reduction in absolute numbers, and particularly the relative decline after 1970, reflected dispersal of industries beyond Keihin to escape locational control in the built up areas.

CHARACTERISTICS OF COMPOSITION BY TYPE OF INDUSTRY

The ratio of heavy and chemical industries is generally regarded as high in Keihin industrial region, the largest centre in Japan. Light industries contribute 30%, and heavy and chemical industries 70% of value added, according to the usual classification (Table 15). This classification, however, presents problems. For example, the manufacture of lipstick cases is classified as heavy industry since the work is metal pressing and further, the lipstick itself, a chemical product, is classified as a chemical industry. However, such products as lipstick, face powder and so on are obviously immediate consumables, and in Keihin region, particularly in Tokyo, its central portion, factories. classified as heavy and chemical industries, but actually producing immediate consumables, form a large part of the total. In the machinery industry, too, many smaller factories have characters different from heavy and chemical industries with enormous plant. Consequently the Keihin region industries are better classified into three, namely, the immediate consumable industries, the assembly-type machinery industries, from radio to motor vehicles, and the heavy and chemical industries, which produce elementary materials proper. On this classification the assembly-type machinery industries account for 48.2% and the immediate consumables industries 34.8%, as shown in Table 15, making them the two largest groups in the region. The Tokyo

TABLE 15

Type of Industrial Composition of Keihin Industrial Region by Value Added, 1973 (in hundred million yen)

		Saitama	Chiba	Tokyo	Kanagawa	Keihin
Grouping to Two	Total	1693 (100.0)	1265 (100.0)	4140 (100.0)	3410 (100.0)	10512 (100.0)
	Light	533 (31.5)	267 (21.1)	1714 (41.1)	523 (15.3)	3031 (28.9)
	Heavy & Chemical	1160 (68.5)	998 (78.9)	2430 (59.6)	2887 (84.7)	7475 (71.1)
Grouping to Three	Immediate Consumables	683 (40.3)	280 (22.1)	2125 (51.3)	569 (16.7)	3657 (34.8)
	Elementary Heavy & Chemicals	137 (8.1)	653 (51.6)	197 (4.7)	799 (23.4)	1786 (17.0)
	Assembly Type Machinery	873 (51.6)	332 (26.3)	1822 (44.0)	2042 (59.9)	5069 (48.2)

Source: Census of Manufacturers.

Prefecture alone has more than half the total percentage of the immediately consumable industry. A high percentage of such industry is characteristic of manufacturing industries in large cities.

In Kanagawa Prefecture the heavy and chemical industries long held high rank, but have been supplanted by the machinery industry, which now exceeds the output of Tokyo. The heavy and chemical industries form a high percentage in Chiba Prefecture, where growth of steel and petroleum chemicals has been remarkable.

COMPONENTS BY SIZE

Table 16, showing factories divided into three groups – those having 300 or more workers, those having 30 to 299 workers, and those having 29 or fewer – brings out considerable differences by area. The small factories (1–29 workers) employ 43% of the total workers in Tokyo Prefecture, which exceeds the national average by 10%, and, further, the majority of these workers belong to the smallest factories (9 or fewer workers).

TABLE 16

Composition by Scale Based on Number of Workers, 1973 Persons (%)

Prefectures	1–29	30–299	More than 300	Total
Saitama	168291 (32.7)	207710 (40.3)	139039 (27.0)	515040 (100.0)
Chiba (Keiyo)	71559 (24.7)	109245 (37.7)	108872 (37.6)	289675 (100.0)
Tokyo	538764 (43.2)	382516 (30.7)	324543 (26.1)	1245823 (100.0)
Kanagawa	135295 (17.3)	209470 (26.8)	438237 (55.9)	783002 (100.0)
Keihin	913909 (32.2)	908941 (32.1)	1010691 (35.7)	2833541 (100.0)

Source: Census of Manufacturers.

For these smallest factories the collection of statistics decreases in effectiveness in the larger cities – in Tokyo for instance, it is probably not more than 60% complete. The table, therefore, underestimates the percentage of total factories provided by this group. On the other hand the percentage of large factories (300 or more workers) is high in Kanagawa Prefecture, with more than half the total workers. Next is Chiba Prefecture, but it exceeds Kanagawa Prefecture in the percentage of factories possessing industrial sites of more than 10 ha. This reflects the fact that capital intensive type factories, employing little labour, are agglomerated in Keiyo region. In Saitama Prefecture employment is relatively strong in factories having 30–299 workers. A characteristic of the region is that smaller factories concentrate in the inner area and large factories locate in the outer ring.

DEVELOPMENT OF INDUSTRY AND EXPANSION OF THE REGION

DEVELOPMENT OF INDUSTRY

Edo, before it became Tokyo, had a population of a million people. Given the demand generated by such a large population, there must have been a considerable amount of industry in Edo. For example, the presence of minor industries such as lumbering, related to the construction of wooden houses, foundry work, thought to occupy more than 50 workshops, lacquer work, related to the sheaths of swords and table wares, furniture, woodwork industry, accessory manufacture, such as tortoise-shell works, is known. There were many kinds of domestic manual work, such as making Japanese umbrellas, round fans, braids and others, which depended on low wage earners and their families. According to the statistics of 1874, Kyoto was the prefecture with the largest industrial production in Japan. Then Osaka, Aichi, Yamaguchi, Tochigi, Nagano, and Niigata followed. Tokyo, with production only about one quarter of that of Kyoto, was ninth. The centre of industrial activities at that time was Hanshin (Osaka-Kobe) region and Keihin ranked low. This situation continued until immediately before World War II.

The Meiji Restoration aimed at the rapid introduction of modernised industry, and government model factories were established in various places. Many were located in Tokyo, the new metropolis, and included factories for manufacturing paper, glass and cement. Most of those factories, however, were ultimately transferred to private enterprise. Other private companies in shipbuilding, cotton spinning, and the manufacture of steam engines and vehicles, were established mainly on the lower fluvial plain of the River Sumida. Around 1900 most large factories in Tokyo were located in the urban fringe.

The industry of Tokyo, however, was not limited to the new factory system production. Domestic workshops, controlled by Toiya (or Tonya),[1] existed in Koto district, and production of consumables such as Western-style umbrellas, decorative articles, clothing, etc., was carried out there. This consumables production is still carried on. At that time, too, the beginnings of the manufacture of machinery, of telegraphic instruments and of machine tools were seen. Many of those industries received technical guidance from government and from the army and the navy, and their dependence on governmental and military demands was high.

On the other hand, export-related industries developed in Yokohama, which grew as an out-port of Tokyo, and the Keihin Canal was constructed for transporting the imported raw materials from Yokohama to Tokyo. In consequence industries depending upon imported raw materials were established along the canal. By about 1910 the Keihin industrial region had almost completed its shaping. Industry in the region in this period was still far below the level of that of the Hanshin region, but a remarkable expansion occurred after about 1930 in the heavy-chemical industries, against the background of expanded military equipment, and Keihin region became the top industrial region by overtaking Hanshin region in 1940, immediately prior to Japanese involvement in World War II (Fig 2.2).

Although its lead shrank somewhat immediately after the War, its industries, characterised by the machinery industry, a growth industry, displayed an astonishing development in the

[1]'Toiya' originally meant merchant wholesaler, but came to mean the lending of raw materials to small operators or paying them commission for production. This antiquated system of controlling production and distribution by commercial interests is called the Toiya system and is very reminiscent of the putting-out system in England and the Verlagssystem in Germany.

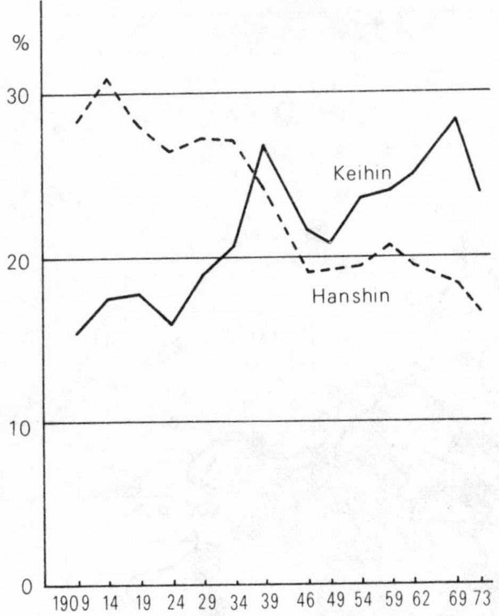

Fig. 2.2 Change of regional share by value. Japan = 100
Source: Census of industrial manufacturers

high economic growth period of the 1960s. Moreover, heavy and chemical industries, related especially to petroleum chemistry and iron and steel, showed remarkable development in the coastal areas of Chiba Prefecture (Keiyo region). After 1970, however, dispersal of factories of large enterprises from the over-agglomeration in the metropolitan area became active, and therefore the relative position of Keihin industrial region tends to decline.

SCOPE OF THE INDUSTRIAL REGION

With the expansion of industrial production in Keihin region, the area of the industrial region expanded substantially.

As Figure 2.3 shows, the average wage per capita in the core of Keihin region is higher than the national average and the machinery industry accounts for over 40% of the total. The core has a radius of 50–60 km, but the machinery industry has been diffusing to outer areas seeking a labour force since the early 1960s. Such dispersed factories are generally located

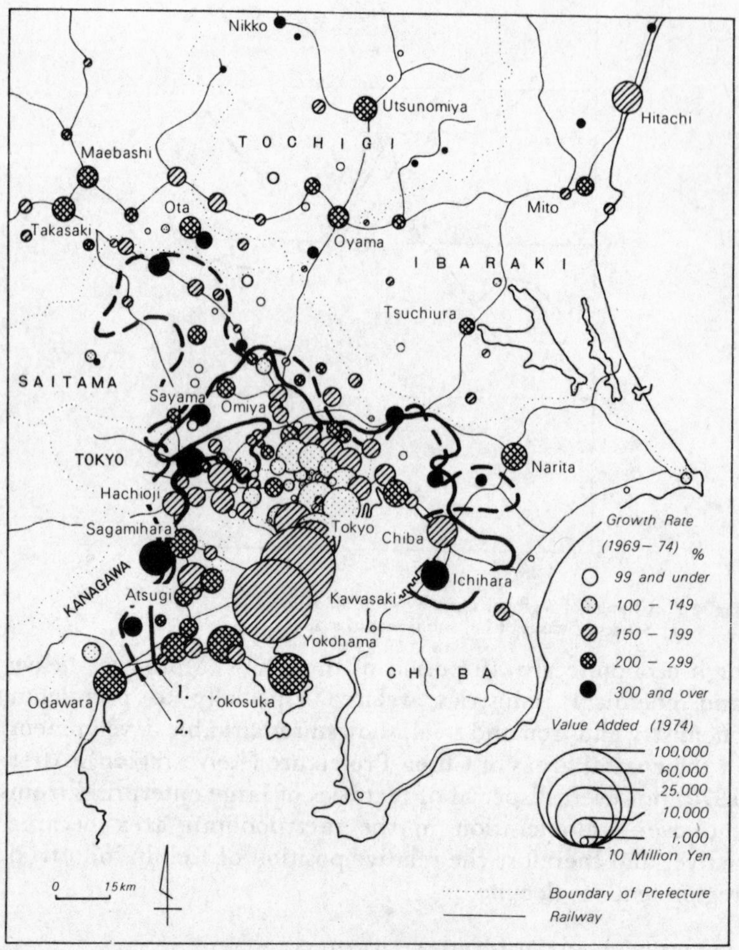

Fig. 2.3 Distribution of manufacturing industry in Kanto region, 1968
Source: Census of industrial manufacturers
1 Sphere in which wage per capita is higher than national average.
2 Sphere in which machinery industry is higher than 40%.

within an 8-hour trip by night truck service from the inner Keihin region. For instance, a large assembly factory of Canon cameras is located in Fukushima city, 300 km north-east of Tokyo. All the parts are brought to the depot in southern Tokyo from sub-contract factories located in its surroundings.

These collected parts are carried to Fukushima by truck, and completed cameras are carried as return cargo. This flow of goods is continuous: there is not a single sub-contractor in the vicinity of Fukushima factory. Northern Kanto and Southern Tohoku are similarly linked with Keihin region. These factories produce high-class cameras by highly-paid workers of great technical skill.

HEAVILY CONCENTRATED AREAS OF INDUSTRY

In order to clarify the areas where industries are particularly concentrated within Keihin industrial region, the writer prepared a density diagram by dotting a mesh-map and by picking up factories having 30 or more workers. The area where five or more factories are located per 1 km^2 was defined as a heavily concentrated area, and almost no change has occurred in its scope over the past ten years. It extends from inner Tokyo to Kawasaki and Yokohama in the south, to southern Saitama Prefecture in the north and to the border of Chiba Prefecture in the east, and contains 60% of the total number of factories in Keihin region. This ratio has fallen by 5% from that of ten years ago. In the western part of Tokyo a small concentration has begun to appear since the 1960s.

In Figure 2.4 the division was made on the criterion that a particular type of industry numbers more than half the total factories in a concentrated area. In the first the machinery industry occupies more than half, in the second it is the heavy and chemical industries and in the third the immediate consumables industry. In the fourth publishing, printing and book-binding provide more than half the total production of consumer goods. Finally, the fifth has no specific industry occupying more than half the total production and is labelled a mixed type.

In location, the machinery district coincides with the southern district in the concentrated area and extends from the south-western district, which includes Sagamihara, Hachioji, Hino and Mitaka to southern Saitama Prefecture. The heavy chemical district concentrates in the coastal areas of Kawasaki and Yokohama. The consumer goods district extends from the eastern district to the borders of Saitama and

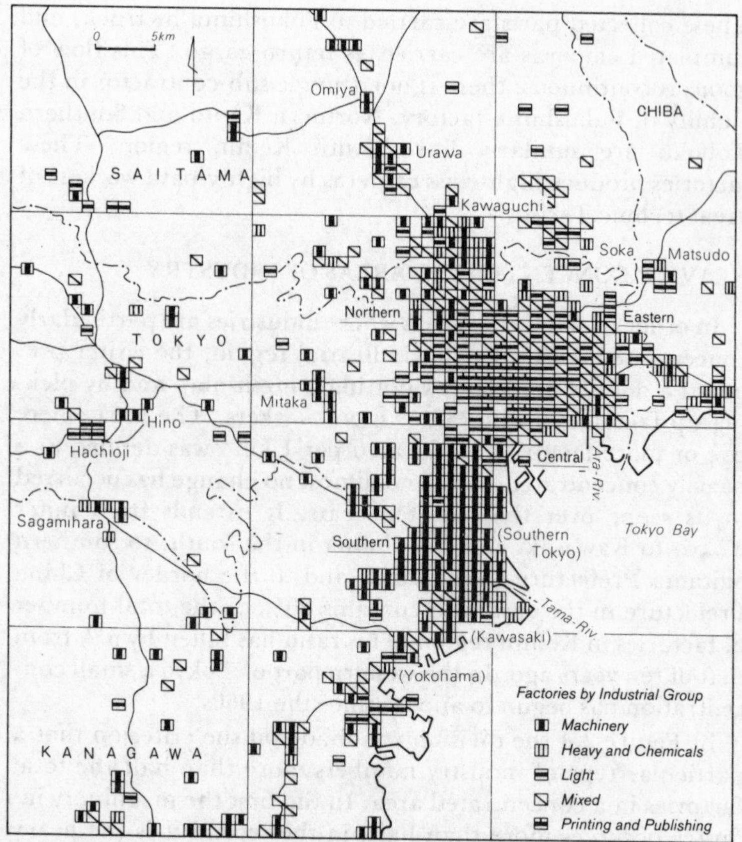

Fig. 2.4 Regional differentiation of Keihin region, 1968
Source: The General List of all factories in Japan

Chiba Prefectures. The publication-printing district coincides with central Tokyo, where various central management functions such as governmental offices and the head offices of various organs are concentrated. The mixed type districts are found in the peripheral portions of the eastern and northern districts. However, included in the heavy chemical or machinery industries in the eastern district are many factories producing such commodities as metal pressings, gears and screws, which are really consumer goods. Expansion of the southern district towards the south-western, which is characterised by the machinery industry, has been remarkable, while the development of its eastern district and the north-eastern district outskirts has been comparatively slow.

THE HEAVY CHEMICAL INDUSTRIAL REGION ALONG THE TOKYO BAY COAST

In the coastal region south of Tokyo, stretching from Kawasaki to Yokohama, and the coastal region of Chiba Prefecture, including Funabashi, Chiba, Kisarazu, Kimitsu and others, are crowded huge factories of iron and steel, petrochemicals, chemistry, shipbuilding, thermal power generation and so on, of impressive appearance. Large factories, however, are not located in Tokyo, currently the centre of Keihin industrial region. There is no more room for constructing large factories in the built-up areas in Tokyo, and such factories have already moved to its outskirts.

It was after Nippon Kokan built its factory early in this century that large heavy and chemical industries began to be located in the Kawasaki-Yokohama coastal region. In this district, not only heavy and chemical factories but also numerous factories of electric machinery, foods and so on were constructed. The newly-born Zaibatsu that forecast the development of this district carried out land reclamation simultaneously with the digging of the canal to induce chemistry, metal, shipbuilding and other firms to locate there. Against this, no canal was dug in the delta on the left bank (Tokyo side) of the River Tama nor was reclamation of land advanced. For this reason location of heavy and chemical industries hardly appeared in southern Tokyo, and fishing villages still remained there until the 1950s. Land has now been reclaimed and various public facilities have been installed, in addition to the Haneda Airport, but industrial utilisation is still slight. On the other hand reclamation of the foreshore was further advanced during the high economic growth period after the War in Kawasaki and Yokohama, which resulted in the appearance of a petrochemical industrial complex of national prominence. In Kawasaki, Nippon Kokan, the second largest iron and steel maker, relocated its existing works on newly reclaimed offshore land and constructed the most advanced blast furnace.

Nippon Kokan has since built a large works in Hiroshima Prefecture, but still regards the Keihin region as an important base.

On the other hand, most of the coast of Chiba Prefecture along Tokyo Bay was shoaling beaches and was the site of seaweed cultivation or coastal fishery. In addition, since it is close to Tokyo, it was a popular sea-bathing resort. It was after the Kawasaki Steel Corporation constructed a blast furnace on the reclaimed land in 1952 that large heavy and chemical industries progressively moved there and the area began to be called Keiyo industrial region. The shoaling beaches were reclaimed one after another by state and/or prefecture policy, and eventually deep-water ports were constructed, which resulted gradually in the preparation of a huge area of industrial land – in fact 70% of the reclaimed land of Tokyo Bay is in Chiba Prefecture. At the southern end of this reclaimed land Nippon Steel Corporation, the largest iron and steel corporation in Japan, constructed the most advanced integrated steel mills. Approximately 7000 ha of land has been reclaimed in Keiyo coastal region during the past 20 years. The rural landscape has been changed completely, there being 1,300 factories.

So the largest industrial base in Japan for iron-steel and petroleum chemistry was established in the coastal region of Tokyo Bay, which includes, for example, the cities of Kawasaki, Yokohama and Chiba. Chiba Prefecture and Kanagawa Prefecture put together provide 16% of the national production of iron and steel, 18% in chemistry and 37% in petroleum/coal products. The huge factories of Nippon Steel, Nippon Kokan, Kawasaki Steel, and the Sumitomo metal works in Kashima district were located here to take advantage of the great market in East Japan centering on Tokyo. As pointed out previously, however, the position of the heavy and chemical industries in Keihin region with respect to the total industrial production is not too high. The share of Chiba Prefecture in the total industrial production, 47%, is high, but that of the whole Keihin region is merely 16%.

DISTRIBUTION OF THE MACHINERY INDUSTRY

The machinery and the immediate consumable goods industries are major components of industrial activities in

Keihin region. In particular, since the 1960s the machinery industry has played a leading part in the development of Keihin industrial region and given the most important impetus to its areal expansion. The Keihin region provides approximately 30% of the national machinery production, and not only is the amount of production very large but the range includes almost every kind of machinery, and technical levels are high.

The machinery industry is widely distributed in the region but there is concentration in the southern district, which extends from southern Tokyo to Kawasaki and Yokohama. Concentration in southern Tokyo, where the machinery industry has concentrated since the Meiji Era, is particularly high (Fig. 2.3). The industry was first established early in the Meiji Era in Ginza-Kyobashi district, which is now the commercial centre of Tokyo, and progressively expanded to the south by reclaiming low-lying land, such as the shores of minor rivers flowing into Tokyo Bay and the shore of the Bay. Development lagged behind, however, in the Tamagawa Delta, which is near the Haneda Airport. It was just before World War II broke out that intense development began. Machinery factories were located in the whole inland part of Kawasaki and Yokohama and the core of the machinery industry consolidated there in the 1960s. In southern and eastern Tokyo various kinds of machinery industry were established, some of them in the 1920s.

In the north district the precision machinery industry has developed, and in the south of Saitama Prefecture a machinery industry has developed from the casting industry. In outer fringe areas, factories moved from the southern district to cover the fringe from the southern outskirts to the western outskirts and small concentrations grew there, initially in the 1960s. Next, its development extended to the northern outskirts from about 1965, especially along main national roads. In any outer fringe district distribution density is still low, but top-class enterprises, such as the motor vehicle factories of Nissan, Isuzu, Hino, Honda, and the factories of leading electrical machinery makers, such as Toshiba, Hitachi, Sony and Nippon Electricity, have been located.

As a result, the position of the southern district in Keihin region in value of production and in number of workers is becoming lower every year. However, the majority of sub-contractors of important machinery makers located in the peripheral district of Keihin region are still concentrated in the southern district, particularly in southern Tokyo. For example, 55% of the sub-contractors of 14 electric machinery factories and 85% of the total of 14 machine tool factories are in the southern district. As mentioned above, the concentration of the parts producers in the southern district is the same as the concentration of sub-contractors of the machinery factories in the entire Keihin region.

The linkage of parent factories and sub-contractors is multi-layered. It is customary for a machine-maker to commit production of parts, even of the same parts, to several producers to raise the quality of parts and lower the cost by the competition among sub-contractors. Parts producers also contract with as many makers as possible to stabilize their business. So, particularly in the Keihin machinery industry, characterised by its production of high class products varied in kind and small in unit, many parts producers maintain their business by sending small amounts of parts to many makers. Sub-contractors (and makers) function in a complex linkage of groups of machine-makers who produce completed products with groups of parts producers. This complex linkage may be classified into several types. The first is the linkage between machine producers and their parts producers, that is, the linkage within the same kind of industry. The second is the diagonal linkage with another kind of machine producer because of the technical features of the parts. The third is the sub-contracted work of completed products. This is a type of production wherein large finished product suppliers commit the production of part of their output to small size finished product producers with their own brands. This type is frequent in the production of machine tools, electrical machinery, cameras, and meters. The large producers maintain their business by utilising the finished products of sub-contractors concentrated in the southern district.

The fourth is the utilisation of secondary sub-contractors, and the parts producers organise their production through their own sub-contractors. In these circumstances, the southern district is still the centre of machine production in

Keihin region. The machinery producers who have large factories in the outer Keihin ring depend upon parts suppliers located in the southern district, which, therefore, is not only the centre of parts production but also functions as the technical centre for the machinery industry.

In Northern Kanto, beyond the Keihin region, the electrical machinery industry linked with the development of copper mines developed in Hitachi; the motor vehicle industry developed in Ota on the basis of aeroplane production during the war; and the traditional fibre industry has been continued in Ashikaga and Kiryu. These industrial cities display strong independence and cannot be included in Keihin region.

THE SPATIAL PRODUCTION SYSTEM OF THE CONSUMER GOODS INDUSTRIES

Consumer goods, originally produced on a small scale, gradually came, with developments in transport and in storage techniques, to be produced on a large scale for supply to remote markets. There are still, however, many instances of small scale consumer goods by family-type management, as, for instance, of bread and cake. Production of goods which may be classified as consumer goods is exemplified by Jiba industry. In Jiba industry small-size enterprises producing the same kind of goods concentrate in a particular area, and the social division of labour for production and distribution is organised within their own group, and Toiya, which controls production and distribution, intervenes there[1]. Jiba industry is established and managed by local capital in each area as a general rule, but they have nationwide and even export markets.

The Tokyo production-distribution system includes groups of processors engaged in manufacturing but not having their own brands; groups of processing-wholesalers, who have processors under them and sell products to those processors; and Toiya, who have governing powers in the phase of distribution. Generally the groups of manufacturers and wholesalers are the leaders in production, which they carry out organising

[1]See footnote, page 52. Accordingly, Jiba industry differs from the so-called local industry or indigenous industry.

a large number of processors. Most of the processors run their businesses from their living accommodation, but when the amount of production increases sufficiently, manufacturers and wholesalers build their own factories, often adequate to accommodate 30 to 100 workers. This type of factory is called a town factory, as distinguished from a large factory operated by industrial capital.

Jiba industries are mainly concentrated in eastern Tokyo. Among them Toiya, who lead productive activities, are concentrated in Nihonbashi and Kanda in central Tokyo, while the processing-wholesalers are concentratzd in Ueno, Asakusa and Hongo in eastern Tokyo, and further the processors are dispersed fanwise in the eastern peripheral portion of Tokyo, which surrounds those areas. They are characterized by production of such goods as handbags, ready-made suits and other kinds of high-class miscellaneous goods in small units. The processors, processing-wholesalers and Toiya must be placed so that they can always maintain close contact with one another. Therefore, the scope for moving the location of a Jiba industry as an urban area or a market expands is limited. Its distribution consequently differs from that of the machinery industry.

COMPOUND INDUSTRIAL AREA AND LIVING–MANUFACTURING MIXED AREA

The southern district, where the machinery industry is concentrated, and the eastern district, where consumer goods industries are concentrated, form a compound industrial area. In the southern district, particularly in southern Tokyo, various machinery factories and their parts manufacturers are concentrated. These factories are linked with the factories in the outer Keihin region, as well as with the factories in the southern district, in a complicated relationship of sub-contract. The sub-contracting relations are multi-layered, and parts manufacturers may further have sub-contractors under their sub-contractors. In the machinery industry, the secondary and the tertiary sub-contractors are in similar circumstances, and they handle mainly metal pressing, plating, machine processing, gears, springs and such items. These items are not merely linked with a few kinds of machine production but are a common element in all machine production, forming a bottom layer of the entire machine industry. These industrial groups are called the bottom groups, en bloc. Almost all the factories in the bottom groups are small, housing not more than 20 workers. Most of them are concentrated in southern Tokyo, the density being particularly high in Ota Ward, adjacent to Kawasaki. The bottom group factories in the southern district deliver their products to parts manufacturers of various kinds of machinery and are complexly linked with other bottom groups.

In southern Tokyo, the eastern district bottom group is strongly linked with the production of consumer goods. In metal pressing, for example, they deliver products such as cigarette lighters, toys, cosmetics, containers, toasters, hairdryers. As mentioned above, inner Tokyo has a complicated organisation, involving Toiya-manufacturers-wholesalers-parts manufacturers in a compound industrial area.

Factory density and population density are particularly high in the compound areas in Tokyo, forming living-manufacturing mixed areas.

Figure 2.5 shows the actual state of a living-manufacturing mixed district in eastern Tokyo. Buildings where living and manufacturing exist together are distributed irregularly. This living-manufacturing mixed area in Metropolitan Tokyo has become a focal point for planned urban redevelopment and consolidation to reduce the risks of fire and earthquake disaster. This kind of living-manufacturing mixed area has generally been considered to represent a chaotic utilisation of land, and policy has been aimed at cleaning up land utilisation by driving out factories. This put the factories in the mixed area in a very difficult situation, but more recently geographers have urged the necessity of reconsideration of the meaning and role of the mixed areas in the activities of a large city, and policy on these mixed areas has been considerably amended.

As a result of some research covering all factories and households in a typical mixed area in inner Tokyo, several characteristics have become clear. Firstly, in every district, manufacturing industry is the most important industry, dominant both in the number of factories and in occupations of householders.

Secondly, there are numerous small factories, occupying tiny sites. Thirdly, factories are located first and dwellings follow, as though they were chasing the factories in those mixed areas. Fourthly, production by, and distribution from, those factories are performed within an extremely limited geographical area. Fifthly, most of the factory owners live at their factories, and most of their dependants work in their factories. The factory workers also live very near the factories. Thus working and living coincide with each other geographically and do not generate the 'commuter rush' of a large city. Sixthly, neither the residents nor the factory owners desire to

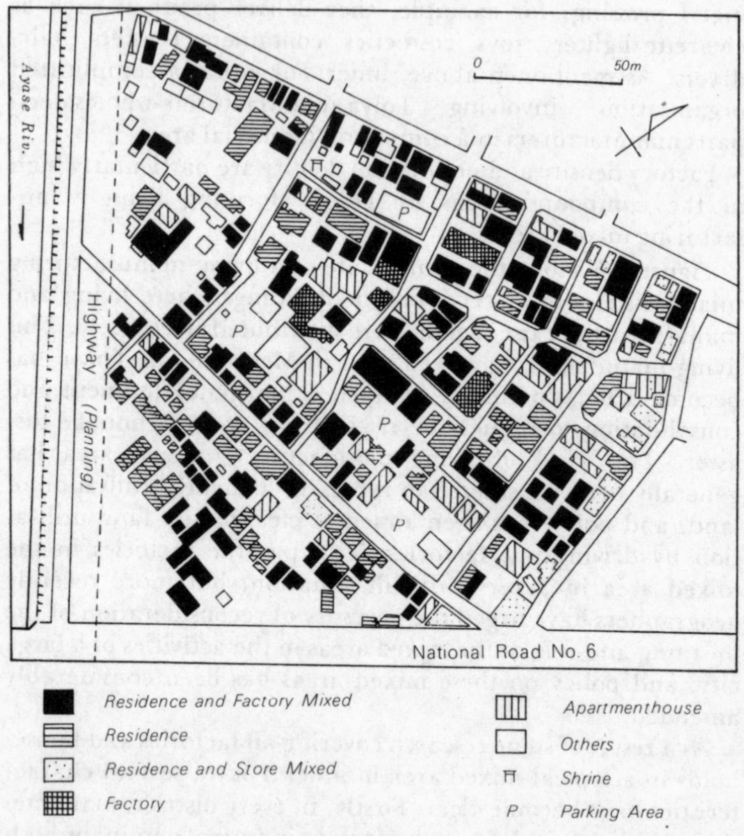

Fig. 2.5 Distribution of houses and factories in eastern Tokyo, 1974

move to any other place but to remain at their present sites. So, the day-time population and the night-time population are about the same in the typical living-manufacturing mixed area. The service industries and retailers also depend upon these residents for maintaining their businesses. This kind of area, then, has a character quite different from that of a residential area, where the night-time population is predominant, or a business area, where the day-time population is predominant, although it is in the same large city. It forms an areal community centering on small-scale manufacturing industries.

2

Chukyo-Tokai Region

I. OTA

CHUKYO INDUSTRIAL REGION

CHARACTERISTICS OF THE REGION

The Nagoya Metropolitan Area, the third largest in Japan, forms the Chukyo Industrial Region. Chukyo means a large city which lies between Kyoto, the old metropolis, and Metropolitan Tokyo, and is another name for Nagoya. The Chukyo industrial region statistically covers the three prefectures of Aichi, Gifu and Mie. These three prefectures plus Shizuoka Prefecture are sometimes called the Tokai region but in this book Shizuoka Prefecture is treated separately and called the Tokai Industrial Region.

A characteristic of Chukyo industrial region is the high percentage of the textile, clothing and transport equipment industries, particularly the production percentage of motor vehicles. In the other two of the three major industrial regions, the Keihin region (Tokyo metropolitan area) has a low production percentage of textiles, and Hanshin region (Osaka metropolitan area) a low percentage of motor vehicles. Chukyo is intermediate between these two.

Output is particularly high in Nagoya, Toyota and Yokkaichi, and these three cities contribute 35% of the region's output (1974). A similar concentration of production in a few specific cities characterises the other industrial regions. In the Keihin region, the 23 wards of Tokyo, Kawsaki and Yokohama account for 47% and in Hanshin, Osaka, Kobe and Sakai 32%, both high ratios.

The three prefectures of Aichi, Gifu and Mie have a total of 195 cities, towns and villages, and 9 urban areas, which include the above-mentioned three cities, providing half the

TABLE 17

Industrial Production in the Chukyo Region*, 1974

Industrial Group	Shipments (100 million yen)	(%)	City of the largest shipment and its proportion to the total
Total	158,992	100.0	Nagoya (17.0%)
Food and kindred products	11,449	7.2	Nagoya (23.2%)
Textiles and clothing products	17,355	10.9	Ichinomiya (8.3%)
Lumber and wood products	7,097	4.5	Nagoya (23.7%)
Pulp, paper and allied products	4,769	3.0	Kasugai (16.7%)
Publishing, printing & allied industries	1,852	1.2	Nagoya (67.4%)
Chemicals and allied products	9,821	6.2	Yokkaichi (36.8%)
Petroleum and coal products	4,445	2.8	Yokkaichi (n.a.)
Ceramic, stone and clay products	9,079	5.7	Nagoya (9.8%)
Iron and steel	12,884	8.1	Tokai (41.9%)
Non-ferrous metals and products	3,687	2.3	Nagoya (40.7%)
Fabricated metal products	7,904	5.0	Nagoya (24.4%)
Ordinary machinery	14,609	9.2	Nagoya (25.3%)
Electrical machinery, equipment & supplies	9,955	6.3	Nagoya (19.1%)
Transport equipment	35,584	22.4	Toyota (47.8%)
Precision instruments	900	0.5	Nagoya (37.4%)
All other industries	7,602	4.7	Nagoya (15.9%)

*Prefectures of Aichi, Gifu and Mie

Source: Census of Manufacturers, 1974

total industrial output. The areas of active industrial production are actually limited to the coastal areas and the areas along the main railways and highways, and most of them lie within 40 km of central Nagoya. Nagoya, the leading producer overall, leads in ten kinds of industry (Table 17), and is first or second in every industry shown in the Table except for textiles and oil refining. It is the core of the Chukyo industrial region, with varied manufacturing industries. The textile industry and the ceramic, stone and clay industry, which have developed over a very long period, do not show any extreme concentration in one city. Publishing and printing industries, typically located in large cities, are concentrated in Nagoya; chemistry and oil refining industries in Yokkaichi; the iron and steel industry in Tokai City, which has the only integrated steel plant in the region; the non-ferrous metal industry in Nagoya, where an aluminium refinery is located; and the transport equipment industry in Toyota, which is Japan's largest centre of the motor vehicle industry.

The concentration of growth industries in certain cities since the 1950s is remarkable.

DEVELOPMENT OF THE REGION

In the Chukyo region, unlike Keihin or Hanshin, modern industrial development was not initiated by any state-managed factory. Accordingly the establishment of heavy industry, which is supported by government demand, was late in starting, and the textile and ceramic industries were important as existing local industries in the early stage of industrialisation. Aichi Prefecture was a centre of cotton cultivation in the Tokugawa Era, and cotton manufacturing was carried on in various places. A few state-managed factories started cotton spinning in tune with the local conditions. The imported spinning machines, however, were not suitable for processing domestic cotton, and moreover cheap raw cotton, imported from India, precipitated a sudden decline of local cotton cultivation. Bisai district in the north-west of Nagoya changed from a cotton textile to a wool textile production centre, as use of western style suits spread after the Russo-Japanese war of 1904-05. So the development of the textile industry also meant the change from domestic raw cotton to imported cotton and wool. They were imported in Yokkaichi City where large factories were built. Fairly soon the textile machinery industry was born to service the textile industry. Sakichi Toyota (who invented automatic weaving machines) and his relatives managed a textile machinery business and spinning and weaving enterprises, and in 1936 started the production of motor vehicles, utilising their engineering techniques. This was the springboard for the creation of today's Toyota kingdom in Chukyo.

Ceramic ware production was active in the inland area north-east of Nagoya, where porcelain clay is produced. Seto, its centre, had nationwide markets and was so famous that the word Seto-mono, or products of Seto, was used to represent ceramic ware. When ceramic ware became an important export product, regional specialisation of processes saw unpainted ware being baked at Seto and final painting performed in Nagoya, where export merchants had their offices. An integrated mill for performing all processes appeared in Nagoya in 1905. Since the process in ceramics is rather simple, the industry did not develop other related industry, even though its production expanded. In comparison with the production of consumer goods represented by textile and ceramic ware, production in the producer goods sector started late. In Aichi Prefecture, where heavy industry had developed, the producer goods sector produced only 20% of total industrial production in 1920, and only 25% even in 1935. The steel industry had been established by 1910, but its scale was too small to satisfy the demands of the local machinery industry. Chukyo had no integrated steel plant until 1960, though it was already a large industrial region. Factories for related metals, machinery, and chemistry were progressively constructed from the later 1930s to the mid-1940s and the percentage of consumer goods dropped temporarily, but the percentage of producer goods declined again after the war and remained at 37% of the total production in 1950. Excluding the industries established to supply military demand, founders of industries in Chukyo region were mainly local entrepreneurs with much less capital than the big Zaibatsu enterprises in Keihin and Hanshin industrial regions. This is one factor in Chukyo region's industry's preference for consumer goods production.

This aspect changed in the late 1950s. An enterprise belonging to the Mitsubishi group, which revived a chemical industry at the old site of the Naval Fuel Depot in Yokkaichi, constructed an oil refinery in 1956 and focused a large petrochemical industrial centre on the refinery. New reclamation of the sea-shore and new construction of industrial bases in Chukyo were started with capital from Tokyo and Osaka. The local entrepreneurs, who were afraid of being overtaken by growth industries and being defeated in the competition with Keihin and Hanshin, aimed at the development of coastal industrial areas along Ise Bay and Chita Bay in Aichi Prefecture and succeeded in establishing an integrated steel plant in Tokai City. With this as a start, large-scale heavy and chemical industries were located. Toyota Motor Corporation, the top local enterprise, concentrated all related industries in Toyota City and its vicinity in this period. The steel plant of Tokai City was located to supply steel to the Toyota Motor Corporation. The remarkable advancement of Chukyo during the high economic growth period was nothing but the development of the motor vehicle industry and its related industries with the Toyota Motor Corporation as the core. East Mikawa area, which is close to Shizuoka Prefecture (the central city is Toyohashi), was designated by the government as a Special Area for Industrial Consolidation in 1963, and Aichi Prefectural authorities reclaimed the sea-coast and prepared industrial land, but so far the expected accomplishment has not been realised.

MAJOR INDUSTRIAL DISTRICTS

a. The Ise Bay Coast. This district is the centre of heavy and chemical industries in Chukyo. Nagoya, located centrally in Chukyo region, shows a diversified industrial structure, which is usual in any large city, and the ratio of consumer goods, such as foods, lumber processing, publishing and printing and daily necessities to producer goods, such as chemical materials, metals and machinery, is 1:2. Most of the large heavy and chemical industries are located in the vicinity of

Nagoya Port. On the western side of the Bay, the bases of the oil refinery, chemicals, and transport equipment are located. In Yokkaichi City, as a centre of petro-chemical industry, the linkage among factories is very tight, but the industries in other cities have no big agglomeration. For instance, there is no mutual relationship among the spinning, glass, shipbuilding and electrical apparatus factories located in the two cities of Tsu and Matsuzaka and their surroundings, nor is there any industrial area where related factories are distributed to surround a large factory. This is an immature industrial area. Chita Peninsula on the east side of the Bay is a coastal industrial area which is expected to supplement, if not replace, Nagoya, where it has become difficult to find further industrial sites, and its future is considered brighter than that of any other district. In addition to large establishments in iron and steel, shipbuilding and oil refining, food factories and lumber processing in the consumer goods sector are expanding their production. Although the coastal belt of Ise Bay is characterised by heavy and chemical industries, many of the factories have little relation with local enterprises. The heavy and chemical industries produce material for sale elsewhere, and the shipbuilding industry imports its component parts from other areas. The Tokai factory of the Nippon Steel Corporation, which supplies the Toyota Motor Corporation, and the Chita works of Idemitsu Oil, which sells fuel to consumers in Chukyo, are exceptional. When the scale of heavy and chemical industries is large, their orientation toward ports becomes much stronger, and those industries have located themselves in the coastal areas of Ise Bay to utilise the infrastructure which was prepared by public investment.

b. Western Mikawa. In Western Mikawa, which is characterised by the motor vehicle industry centred on Toyota City, many related industries are coupled together functionally, with the motor vehicle assembly plants on the top. As mentioned in Part One, Chapter 4, the Japanese motor vehicle industry has a multifold sub-contract system and any enterprise with an assembly department controls a great number of medium and small enterprises directly and indirectly. This tremendous group of factories is concentrated in Western Mikawa, and their output includes numerous industrial products which are not classified as transport equipment in statistics but which are actually motor vehicle parts. A spinning/weaving industry developed in an old cotton-producing centre, and the techniques in manufacturing automatic weaving machines developed by a local inventor were applied to the manufacturing of motor vehicles with great success. This series of processes produced a new industry out of a preceding industry, with a superior entrepreneur as midwife. There is a character of indigenousness in Chukyo region which cannot be seen in other industrial regions started by state-managed factories and Zaibatsu enterprises, and in Western Mikawa the circumstances are different from the west coast of Ise Bay where new and old industries are operated in the same area with no mutual relationship. Toyota City was formerly called Koromo; it was renamed Toyota City in recognition of the fame of the Toyota Motor Corporation. When you refer to the motor vehicle industry in Chukyo, the name of Toyota is mentioned first, but this area is also a production base of motor vehicle factories of the Mitsubishi group.

c. Bisai. This area, north-west of Nagoya, with Ichinomiya its central city, has an active textile industry. Since the demands for textiles are very varied, production is of numerous kinds and in small quantities. Medium and small are, accordingly, normal enterprises. Since this was originally an agricultural area and the production of cotton cloth was part of the farmers' job, high-level weaving skill has been inherited. The original scale of management was extremely small, but the distribution mechanism for yarn and finished products had already been set up. With modernisation and the decline in demand for cotton cloth for Japanese style garments, it was easy to change over to the production of cloth for western style clothing. The raw material was supplied to weavers from wool spinning factories in Yokkaichi through Toiya, and the finished product delivered to markets again through Toiya. Weavers had the yarn dyed as necessary by committing the work to dyers, very often via Toiya. This complicated mechanism of distribution and production may have prevented advancement in productivity but it gave a means of income to many people. Unlike the coastal industrial areas, Bisai gives no grand view of many large factories. There are some large textile factories in Ichinomiya City, but in most cases many small factories are located among ordinary dwelling houses, merchants' houses, and farmers' houses. The total value of production, however, is huge, the largest in Japan. This area, too, like Western Mikawa, was reborn as a new industrial area by conversion from indigenous industry, but increase of production has been slow, since wool textiles are no longer a growing sector. Proximity to Nagoya, with high land prices accompanying residential development, is an obstacle to future industrial development in this area.

RELATIONSHIP WITH KEIHIN AND HANSHIN

The Chukyo industrial region is located between the two leading industrial regions of the nation, Keihin and Hanshin, and its development has always lagged behind that of these pioneer regions, but it is not far from large markets, and production here did not stagnate, as it did in Northern Kyushu where petroleum replaced coal as the source of energy. The textile, ceramics, and motor vehicle industries can supply their products to other areas because they have raw materials production and cognate industries within the region. However, the machinery industry, except motor vehicles, in which value added is high, must obtain raw materials and other materials from the Keihin and Hanshin industrial regions. The shipbuilding yards located along the coasts of Ise Bay and Chita Peninsula and the electrical apparatus factories in the inland areas have to import steel material and various parts from Keihin and Hanshin. Further, since the labour force supply areas for Chukyo region overlap with those for Keihin region in East Japan and with those for Hanshin region in West Japan, there is severe competition for young workers. Chukyo competes with Hanshin in Kyushu for female workers in the textile industry in particular. Chukyo's position astride the labour market areas of Keihin and Hanshi makes it very difficult for medium and small enterprises to secure labour of good quality.

FUTURE PROBLEMS

Environmental pollution is serious in the coastal areas of Chukyo, where industrial development was concentrated into a short period. In Yokkaichi air pollution has been serious since around 1960, when the petro-chemical industrial complex started operations. A respiratory illness, called Yokkaichi asthma, increased rapidly after 1962 since houses and factories were densely concentrated in a small area. Chimneys were heightened as a countermeasure, with the unanticipated result that the pollutant and the environmental deterioration spread further, up to 5 km from the factories. (Similar phenomena occur around iron works.) At present the petro-chemical industry in Yokkaichi is merely one of the many industrial complexes in Japan. It employs only a small labour force compared with the scale of production, and has no large local market. Clearly the environmental problem requires the reconsideration of the presence of an industry which merely utilises the land and port at the expense of the local communities.

Another problem is the limitation of industrial water sources. The Aichi Canal, originally installed for agricultural purposes, came to be used for industrial activities, and the water of other rivers as industrial water in competition with rice-field irrigation. Iron and steel and chemicals are typical heavy users of water, and therefore further expansion of these industries would inevitably suppress agriculture. It would also come into conflict with the domestic water consumption of the large urban area of Nagoya. Hanshin is making efforts to solve the water problem by all-over utilisation of Lake Biwa, but there is no lake or swamp that can be utilised in Chukyo, and investment large enough to be effective would seriously raise water costs.

TOKAI INDUSTRIAL REGION

CHARACTERISTICS OF THE REGION

This region is sandwiched between the two large urban areas of Tokyo and Nagoya and extends east and west along the Tokaido Railway. The administrative division coincides with Shizuoka Prefecture. According to the 1974 statistics, the value of industrial shipments of the prefecture was 5.3 billion yen, which puts it sixth in national shipments. This is about half the value of that for Tokyo, but it far exceeds Fukuoka (Northern Kyushu), formerly a large industrial prefecture.

In Fig. 2.6, which shows the composition of industry, numbers 4–9 for Shizuoka Prefecture show up as higher than the national average. This is because the percentage production of pulp, paper and musical instruments (which fall under 'others' in classification) and chemicals is large. On the other hand, oil refining and iron and steel are relatively low-rated. So the graph contrasts with that of Kanagawa prefecture, which is strong in heavy and chemical industries, and the central protrusion is larger than in the national total. The fact that

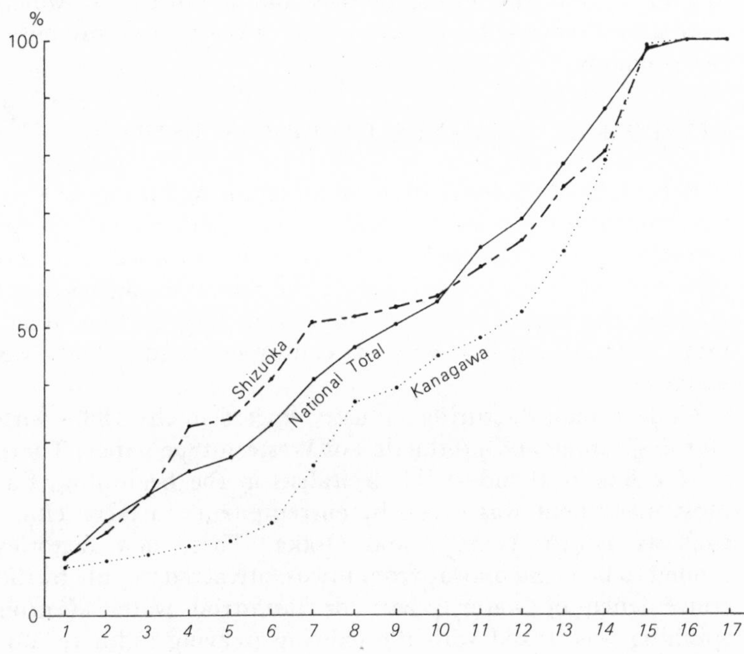

1 *Food and Kindred Products*
2 *Textiles and Apparel Products*
3 *Lumber and All Wood Products*
4 *Pulp, Paper and Allied Products*
5 *Publishing, Printing and Allied Industries*
6 *Other Light Industries*
7 *Chemicals and Allied Products*
8 *Petroleum and Coal Products*
9 *Ceramic, Stone and Clay Products*
10 *Iron and Steel*
11 *Nonferrous Metals and Products*
12 *Fabricated Metal Products*
13 *Ordinary Machinery*
14 *Electric Machinery, Equipment and Supplies*
15 *Transport Equipment*
16 *Precision Equipments*
17 *Ordnance and Accessories*

Fig. 2.6 **Relative situation of the Tokai industrial region, 1974**
Source: Census of manufacturers

Shizuoka Prefecture shows a marked bulge in the last (the right side, Nos. 14–15) comes from the weight of the transport equipment contribution. As mentioned above, Tokai industrial region is still strong in consumer goods production. Among those of particularly high production are the canning of fish and mandarin oranges, tea curing, and the manufacture of velveteen, corduroy, various kinds of paper and pianos. Pianos reach almost 99% of the national production. In addition, aluminium, paper-making machines, lumbering machines, and chemicals, textiles and motor-cycles, which have shown remarkable growth in recent years, are representative products.

DEVELOPMENT OF MANUFACTURING INDUSTRY

Before the Meiji restoration, manufacturing industries were not concentrated in any particular area of this region, except cotton textiles in the west, wood works in Shizuoka City and Japanese paper manufacturing in the mountain agricultural villages, the region being isolated from large urban areas. Other manufacturing was of consumer goods, and was scattered.

Modern manufacturing industry started in the 1880s with cotton spinning and production of Western-type paper. There were a few local industrial capitalists in the beginning, but most investment was made by entrepreneurs in large cities, such as Tokyo, Nagoya and Osaka. These new factories tended to be located away from towns, attracted mainly by the convenience of water power or industrial water. Cotton spinning was linked with the existing weaving industry, but Western-type paper manufacturing was developed with no relation to existing industries. For both industries techniques were imported from Europe and America and, since each completed the whole manufacturing process, they did not generate any related local industry.

In the later 1890s, however, silk reeling was begun by new local entrepreneurs, stimulated by the growth in raw silk exports. Then paper manufacture was also mechanised by local entrepreneurs. Most of them had previously managed small local banks and invested their accumulated capital in the new industries. These two industries developed greatly in the prosperous period during World War I, and indeed in machine-processed Japanese paper production the region rose to the first position in Japan. Industrial development based on local capital had become characteristic of the region. Dissemination of small motors and readiness to undertake production of any commodity already provided by big enterprises provided the conditions for expanding local minor manufacturing industries. Eventually the rise of the paper-making industry invited the development of a paper-making machinery industry.

The outbreak of World War II converted these consumer goods industries to military-demand industries. In the 1940s factories were dispersed to this region from the Keihin industrial region, and gave an impetus to the development of the machinery industry after the war, in particular for the development of electrical apparatus and transport equipment.

The boom initiated by the Korean War revived all the industries of the region except silk reeling. In particular the revival of the textile, paper and wood processing industries, which required relatively little capital investment and provided easy profits, was fast. When the rapid growth of the Japanese economy steadied in the later 1950s, large industries with large fixed capital continued to progress, benefitting from a developed infrastructure. Tagonoura Port, constructed below Mt. Fuji, was welcomed as consolidation of the conditions for accelerating industrial development in this region, where Shimizu had been the only port. It was, for instance, the existence of this port that decided the Asahi Chemical Co. to accept the invitation of the local authorities and locate its synthetic textile works in this region.

In the region as a whole, however, there are still few harbour-oriented industries. After 1960 new factories were constructed successively in the inland areas, where development had previously lagged. Rice-fields, plateaus, forest or lower areas of Mt. Fuji along National Road No. 1 and the Tokaido Railway, which are trunk traffic routes, became desirable industrial areas, although they had no port, and the agricultural landscape changed rapidly. Many of the enterprises coming to this region were relocated there because expansion had become difficult in Keihin region. Expansion of some local enterprise factories does exist, but local capital enterprises no longer lead in the industrialisation process, in which industry is becoming increasingly diversified.

MAJOR INDUSTRIAL AREAS

a. Eastern Surugawan area. This area in the lowlands below Mt. Fuji centres on Fuji City and Numazu City and is outstanding in its consumption of industrial water. Typical water-consuming industries, including pulp and paper, chemicals, textiles, and photographic film, were located to utilise underground water, but in order to prevent ground subsidence by excess pumping, water sources are now being changed to rivers. This is the area where modern industry is concentrated and good examples are seen here of manufacturing industries developed by local landlords and rich merchants. Although production is now mainly in the hands of big enterprises of central capital, leading companies in Japan have been born in the area manufacturing paper and paper-making machinery, and their market controlling power is still strong.

Following the construction of Tagonoura Port and designation as an Area for Industrial Consolidation, large factories increased, especially around 1960. With the expansion of industrial production came the problem of different conditions for industrial enterprise among cities, towns and villages, and a sweeping amalgamation of towns and villages was carried out in order to reduce the disparities. Fuji City, a typical example, was created by the amalgamation of many towns and villages. Such regional alteration of locally autonomous bodies for the convenience of industrial activities is not rare in Japan. Similarly, public control of pollution is being extended. In this area for instance, concentration of pulp and paper making industries brought about not only land subsidence and change of underground water into salt water but also water pollution from drainage. So public industrial water supply systems and drainage systems have been constructed as countermeasures.

b. Shizuoka and Shimizu. In Shizuoka City, which has local government, lumber processing industries for making lacquer wares, dressing tables, furniture and Japanese-style shoes are concentrated. These are products of minor enterprises but the amount of production and of overseas exports is large. Lacquer ware, however, is losing its markets to synthetic resin products, because its techniques are complex and costs of production are high. Another Jiba industry, tea processing, is also carried on by mainly medium and small-size enterprises, though there are some large modern factories in this field.

There are many large-scale industries in Shimizu, which has an international trade port. Aluminium refining, oil refining and shipbuilding, which were developed to meet military demand, are managed by big enterprises. What characterises the industries of Shimizu, however, are not these huge factories but the food industry, which has developed from the canning of mandarin oranges, bonito and tuna and the related industries, particularly manufacturing of tins and cardboard cases. Shizuoka Prefecture is a leading orange-producing area, and canning has been active since the 1920s. In winter, when canning work is busiest, many female workers come to this prefecture from agricultural villages in snowy districts, mainly Niigata. The combination of mandarin orange cultivation, fishery and seasonal workers assisted the canning industry and other food processing industries in this region. In these food processing industries the techniques and processes are comparatively simple and the products are very numerous, making them appropriate to the prevailing medium and small size enterprises. In contrast, can-making factories are managed by the two largest manufacturers in Japan, and the cardboard case factories by the top producer in Japan.

c. Hamamatsu and its neighbourhood. Hamamatsu, like Shizuoka City, was once a castle town but no traditional urban industry developed. The industry which did exist in the area was the cotton textile industry of the agricultural villages. Textile production is still distributed in the surroundings of Hamamatsu, managed mainly be medium and small enterprises, and numerous factories are seen in agricultural villages. The industry as a part-time occupation of agricultural villages, however, is no longer the main force of production. Even a small workshop standing among tea fields operates as a modern industry, obtaining employees from Kyushu and purchasing cotton from large spinning factories in Hamamatsu.

Representative growth industries of the Hamamatsu area

are piano and motor cycle manufacture. The world-famous Honda, Suzuki and Yamaha are all enterprises born in this area, and their bases of production are also located in Hamamatsu and neighbouring cities. Production of pianos increased rapidly because of the rise in incomes and the importance given to the use of musical instruments in school education. Associated with the textile industry, production of weaving machinery is also important.

Since urbanisation was slow in this area, except in Hamamatsu, obtaining industrial sites was comparatively easy in the period of industrial development after the 1960s. In particular, the woods on the diluvial plain were cleared for large factories. Although the development of industrial cities is delayed except in Hamamatsu, the rate of increase of industrial production is extremely high and development of an assembly industry sector is expected. Future development will be difficult, however, in Shimizu, which is proud of its large production value in heavy and chemical industries, since plains land is scanty, but it has port facilities.

3

Hanshin Region

T. FUJIMORI

The industrial region centring on Osaka sometimes means a comparatively narrow area indicated by the term Hanshin (Osaka-Kobe) Region from the viewpoint of regional agglomeration of industries, and sometimes a wider area, Keihanshin (Kyoto-Osaka-Kobe) Region. In either case its centre is Osaka. The areal scope of Hanshin region includes the area from Kobe to Akashi along the Osaka Bay in the west, the coastal area in the vicinity of Sennan City in the south, and further the area in the vicinity of Takatsuki City, which extends inland along the River Yodo.

In the Hanshin industrial region, according to the statistics of Osaka Prefecture and Hyogo Prefecture, the number of establishments is 13.5% of the nationwide figure, persons engaged 14.1% and the production value 7.9%. These figures imply that here the ratio of medium and small enterprises is high, although it is a great industrial region. In output, the highest ratio is provided by iron and steel (26%), second is metal products (25%), and third machinery (21.8%). Industries with more than 10% of the nationwide figures are textiles, chemistry, electrical machinery and equipment and food.

Among the main industrial areas in Japan, this region is characterised as the place where politics, economics and culture developed earliest. In particular, Kyoto had long been the site of the Imperial Palace before the Meiji Era. Osaka, located on the Seto Inland Sea, was a gate for the inland areas and prospered as a centre of traffic and commerce. Even under the Shogunate government in the Tokugawa Era, it was said that the political centre was Edo (Tokyo) and the economic centre was Osaka, and various industries were developed there. For example, textiles (Nishijin brocade), porcelain and many other handicraft articles were produced in Kyoto for the Imperial Household and peers, and in Osaka, where industries necessary in daily living were active. Comparatively large cities had grown in Osaka's peripheral areas, and the neighbouring villages farmed agricultural areas of high productivity. This historically conditioned background was of immense importance when introduced in the Meiji Era. Further, the Japanese traditional industries, now distributed nationwide, owe much to this region.

FORMATION OF HANSHIN INDUSTRIAL REGION

The development of modern industries in this region started around the end of the 1890s. In the beginning government factories played an important role. Among them, the Osaka Artillery Arsenal (1879) became the foundation for metal and machinery industries, the Hyogo Shipbuilding Arsenal (1883) for the modern shipbuilding industry and the Osaka Mint, instituted in 1879, for the metal industry and the chemical industry. Since the region was a cotton-producing area, too, a government spinning mill was established in 1870 in Sakai, south of Osaka. In Osaka, where various kinds of daily necessity goods had long been produced, the production of soap, Western-style umbrellas, matches, cosmetics, brushes, bricks and so on was transferred to the factory system.

The contribution of the textile industry, mainly cotton spinning, to the development of capitalism in Japan is well illustrated by Osaka. Spinning, a private enterprise established in 1883, used steam power from the beginning and introduced electric lighting and night shifts. Many other modern spinning mills were also established by the private capital of feudal lords, landlords, Toiya agents and others, and formed the foundation for the modern industry of Osaka. Other manufacturing industries were started by private capital in cement, sugar, steel and glass, and the rubber industry concentrated in Kobe. These industries expanded their markets on the continent of Asia, which was thrown open by the Sino-Japanese War of 1894–95 and the Russo-Japanese War of 1904–05. In Hanshin region, around the end of the Meiji Era, many small domestic industries still existed, but mechanised processing industry such as the textile industry was firmly established and the region became the largest industrial area in Japan. Heavy and chemical industries were developed by the government to cater for the national market, but control and development were gradually taken over by private capital. Representative of the factories established at that time were the government factory, Hyogo Shipbuilding Arsenal, which was transferred to private enterprise and became a shipbuilding yard of Kawasaki Zaibatsu, and private capital shipbuilding yards started by Mitsubishi and Nomura Zaitbatsu. Thus shipbuilding became a major sector of industry in Hanshin region. In 1889 Sumitomo established a copper wire mill and production of steam trains and aluminium, among others, followed. In the field of chemistry Mitsui constructed a celluloid factory in 1907, and the rubber factories of foreign capital such as Englum and Dunlop and the Toyo Tire of Japanese capital, were built during the period 1908–10.

So the Hanshin region was equipped as an all-inclusive industrial area in the latter half of the Meiji Era, and its coastal area was developed, mainly from Osaka towards Kobe.

The region developed rapidly during World War I. Production for domestic markets was expanded because of the difficulty of importing from European countries during the war, and, further, Japanese merchandise expanded its markets in those areas which had been markets of European countries. Cotton spinning and the manufacture of cotton and knitted goods increased in the farming villages surrounding Osaka, and exports of cotton yarn increased to Asian countries, which had been British markets. Knitted goods also expanded domestic markets by taking the place of imported products. With Asian countries such profitable markets, Kobe and Osaka developed as the ports of shipment for these products. In particular the development of Kobe was remarkable, until it is now one of the two greatest trading ports in Japan, competing with Yokohama.

The heavy and chemical industries also began to grow in this period, with production of steel, copper, aluminium and machinery increasing, and the manufacture of household electrical equipment started by leading Japanese enterprises such as Mitsubishi Electrical Corporation and Matsushita Electrical

Industrial Company. Sakai developed its bicycle industry until now it has a nationwide market. The heavy chemical industry did not develop, since there was not sufficient electrical power, but industries related to medical supplies, industrial chemical products, dyes and others, developed. With the establishment of large factories, the medium and small enterprises that had earlier been located inside the city became sub-contractors of the big enterprises, which promoted remarkable development of the daily necessity goods industry, in the medium and small-size cities around Osaka as well as in Osaka itself. Some characteristic districts were formed which specialised in specific products such as artificial pearls, spectacle lenses, fountain pens, Western style umbrellas and so on. So the outline of Hanshin industrial region was about completed by World War I. Into it came workers from remote agricultural areas such as Kyushu, Chugoku or Shikoku. Houses for workers were built side by side in inner Osaka, and Osaka became the most densely populated area together with Tokyo. Railways and roads were also built from Osaka outwards to Kyoto, Kobe and Wakayama. Further satellite towns began to be formed in the outskirts of Osaka for people employed in Osaka.

Considerable fluctuation occurred in the industrial characteristics of Osaka from early in the Showa Era to the outbreak of World War II. With the expansion of the munitions industries the textile and household goods industries were dispersed from Osaka to peripheral areas of Osaka, to Tokai region and to more distant places, or were converted into munitions industries. The textile industry had occupied the central position in the industrial modernization of Osaka, but had considerably declined by the end of this period. On the other hand, heavy industries such as metals and machinery expanded but did not reach nationwide stature, and they declined relatively to Keihin, which made great progress in this period.

Towards the end of World War II, raw materials, power and labour were all in short supply and in addition the Hanshin industries became paralysed by air-raids. Economic restoration was not easy after the war ended, but medium and small enterprises producing daily necessities began to recover after 1947. The regulations limiting cotton spinning were abolished in 1950 and Hanshin quickly became the world's chief exporter by value of cotton cloth. Other industrial production industries which had been diverted to munitions industries and heavy industry were also gradually converted to peace industry and the light industrial sector, and in consequence the ratios of textiles and food industries rose. In spinning and textiles, however, Chukyo's percentage increased, and the newly-born synthetic fibre industry was not located in Hanshin. The relative position of Hanshin, therefore, in the national textile industry remained much lower than before the war, and the ratios of the machinery and metal industries which were continued after the war improved somewhat.

TABLE 18

Value of Industrial Shipments in the Hanshin Industrial Region*, 1974

	Value of Shipments (100 million yen)	Percent
Total	228,435	100.0
Food and kindred products	22,290	9.8
Textiles	18,943	8.3
Lumber and wood products	6,807	3.0
Pulp, paper and allied products	7,292	3.2
Publishing, printing and allied industries	6,265	2.7
Chemicals and allied products	18,071	7.9
Petroleum and coal products	6,332	2.8
Ceramic, stone and clay products	5,806	2.5
Iron and steel	32,227	14.1
Non-ferrous metals and products	8,794	3.8
Fabricated metal products	18,407	8.1
Ordinary machinery	26,354	11.5
Electrical machinery, equipment and supplies	20,904	9.2
Transport equipment	13,767	6.0
Precision instruments	2,158	0.9
All other industries	14,017	6.2

* Prefectures of Osaka, Kyoto and Hyogo
Sources: Census of Manufacturers, 1974

In 1950, the Korean War brought about a special procurement boom, but Hanshin suffered a heavy blow in the industries related to fibre, bicycles, medical supplies, optical equipment, tools and others through the loss of the pre-war Chinese market. By the later 1950s these products had to be exported to the United States and south-eastern Asia, but in exports to these markets Hanshin compared badly with Keihin, and Kobe Port lost ground relatively.

Even in the period when the heavy and chemical industries were developing rapidly through innovation, the locational conditions of Hanshin were not favourable to the growth of new types of industries. Not only did old factories have no room for expansion and the city have few industrial sites for location of new factories, but also ground subsidence was progressive and factories began to migrate from inner Hanshin. So inner Hanshin was relatively depressed and industries expanded toward the peripheral areas of Osaka.

DEVELOPMENT OF OUTER HANSHIN

The New Coastal Area. Approximately 2,300 ha of marine surface was reclaimed along Osaka Bay from the southern part of Osaka Harbour to the vicinity of Kishiwada City, including Sakai City, and 108 establishments including iron and steel, steam-power stations, shipbuilding, oil refining and petroleum chemistry, are now located here, forming a new industrial complex. This district is called the Sakai-Senhoku district, which has approximately 22,000 employees and shipments of approximately 1.1 billion yen. On the other hand, in Harima district, west of Kobe, an industrial site exceeding 1,000 ha was reclaimed and more than thirty large factories (steam-power stations, iron and steel, heavy machinery and chemistry) are located there. The industrial development in these coastal areas was aimed at stemming the decrease of economic power in Hanshin region by developing these areas as a new industrial city. Newly built factories introduced innovation and high productivity, and formed an important district in Hanshin region, but its scale is small, only about one-third of the new development around Tokyo Bay.

The East District. The inland area east of Osaka City is characterised by the dominance of numerous medium and small size enterprises, and dwellings and factories are mixed. The industry in this area is of two types. One is the machinery and metal-working factories of sub-contractors and/or related firms of large factories located in the coastal areas; the other is the industries with a long history of production of daily necessity goods such as are characteristic of Osaka City. In particular, the manufacture of various kinds of products suitable for urban life, carried on under the domestic production system before the Meiji Era, continued to grow even after it. Characteristic products are vacuum flasks, artificial pearls, spectacle lenses, hair-clippers, celluloid products, artificial flowers, fountain pens and Western-style umbrellas. These industries, characterised by medium and small firms, started their recovery very quickly after World War II.

The North District. This district extends north of Osaka City along the River Yodo. There were textile, chemistry, food and other factories before World War II, and after the war the electrical machinery and equipment works which already existed in Moriguchi and Kadoma developed very suddenly. The most conspicuous advances were shown by the factories producing household electrical equipment. Sanyo, Matsushita, Sharp and Mitsubishi, for example, constructed most advanced factories here. In addition, factories for producing daily necessity goods such as beer, foreign-style liquor, cake and candies, tobacco, underwear and canned foods, stand side by side along the railways and national highways from Osaka to Kyoto.

For a view of the relations between industrial development in agricultural areas and local communities the case of Matsushita Electrical Industrial Company in Kadoma City is interesting. Kadoma City was an agricultural area, on almost wholly low and moist land, with hosiery processing – originated late in the Meiji Era – as its only industry. Of the surplus labour force, men commuted to the artillery factory and women to hosiery and textile factories in Osaka City.

In 1933 the Matsushita Electrical Industrial Company built its factory here. The company, which had started with a town factory in Osaka City, planned to relocate in a suburban area where land value was low. The landlords in Kadoma City also worked for the introduction of the factory, and the Kadoma location was decided on. After World War II, Matsushita seized the opportunity of the increase of demand for household electrical equipment. It enlarged its factory every year, increased its range of products, made the area centering on Kadoma the base for its main office, research and production, and grew to be a leading electrical appliance maker in Japan. The company now has numerous factories throughout Japan, including Keihin. Among the reasons for the company's success in developing from Kadoma as its base are, first, that it efficiently organised a sub-contracting production system and, second, that it absorbed the surplus labour in the agricultural villages in and around this district at low wages. Beyond this, it also attracted urban wage earners from Osaka City.

Nara District. Another place where industry pushed into the inland area is Nara. Nara is surrounded by mountains and, with water in short supply, development of modern industry was late in starting. After the Nagoya-Osaka highway was opened and the motorway between Nara and Kyoto, Wakayama City, and other peripheral cities was completed, factories for machinery, electrical and other precision apparatus, chemicals, foods and so on were established, mainly from Osaka to the Nara area, centering on Yamato-Koriyama City, the nodal point. Nara Prefecture, however, has a limited labour supply and many cultural relics, and so development of industrial sites must be limited. Nara, consequently, is more likely to be developed as a residential and recreation area for Hanshin people.

Kyoto-Biwa Lake District. This industrial area extends outward from Hanshin industrial region to include the area from Kyoto to Biwa Lake (Shiga Prefecture).

Kyoto, for long the metropolis of Japan, had superior traditional industries. The most famous silk textile, Nishijin brocade, was produced in a concentrated district of small handicraft industrialists in the city, and numerous dyers were also present. Yuzen print, utilising the water of the city's river, was also well known. Kiyomizu porcelain and Japanese *sake* (spirit) were also marketed throughout the country. In the Meiji Era, while Osaka was modernising its industry, Kyoto continued the production of artistic products by traditional manual techniques. After World War I, however, those techniques were gradually modernised, and the manual emphasis is now weakening. Along with technical improvements, management was also modernised. The Kiyomizu porcelain factory has moved from Kyoto City to a suburban estate and is introducing new methods. Besides these traditional industries, factories for electrical apparatus, machinery and metal work are located in the southern district of Kyoto City and linked with outer Osaka. Textiles such as linen and silk were long produced along the shores of Lake Biwa, the largest lake in Japan, approximately 700 km^2 in area, utilising the abundant water supply, and the first rayon factory in Japan was located there in the 1920s. Further modern factories followed, and many synthetic fibre factories are now sited along the south shore of the lake, making the area a nationally important centre of the synthetic fibre industry.

The river flowing from Lake Biwa to Osaka early made water transport from and to Lake Biwa important in the economic development of Kyoto and Osaka. The contribution of water transport decreased with the opening of the railways, but the lake has continued to furnish water for domestic and industrial use. The value of Lake Biwa's water was indeed heightened when pumping up of underground water had to be limited because of ground subsidence in Osaka.

At present the comprehensive development of Lake Biwa is planned as a national project, aimed mainly at supplying water to Osaka and Hyogo Prefectures. However, supplying large quantities of water would threaten danger to fisheries, agriculture, drinking water and the landscape, as well as to the synthetic textile industry – for which the abundant water was the locating factor – since the water level becomes extremely low during the winter. Since, however, there is no other water source in the Hanshin region, these risks have to be accepted, though equitably adjusting the advantages and disadvantages will be very difficult.

Hanshin region is the oldest industrial area in Japan and, in built-up areas, number of establishments, number of workers and value of shipments per unit area, surpasses Tokyo. When industrial agglomeration in the inner areas reached its limits in the early 1960s, industries spread out to the peripheral areas, but these outer areas have also now reached their limits. Pumping of underground water is sternly restricted because of ground subsidence, and it is difficult to obtain a new water source. Environmental pollution by industrial activities has not been satisfactorily solved.

The Hanshin region has declined relative to Tokyo. A

comparison of comprehensive economic power, including manufacturing industry, commerce and finance, gave Osaka's percentage of Tokyo's as 67.3 in 1960 and only 61.1 in 1972. The reason for the efforts made to develop the heavy and chemical industries by large-scale reclamation in the 1960s was to reverse this decline, but in the result the Keihin region realised a larger development.

The relative decline of the economic power of Hanshin region, particularly that of Osaka, is not simply an industrial problem. The main cause is that the Osaka financial enterprises moved their main offices to Tokyo, taking advantage of the new data communication systems and/or the introduction of the super express trains.

What would be required to restore Osaka's position is the nurturing of industries with high value added, the transfer of some of the central political and economic management functions from Tokyo to Osaka, and the provision of facilities appropriate to an international trade centre, such as the new international airport now being planned.

PART THREE

Other Industrial Regions

1

Setouchi and Northern Kyushu Region

T. FUJIMORI

SETOUCHI (SETO INLAND SEA) INDUSTRIAL REGION

The southern part of Chugoku region, which runs east-west, and the northern coast of Shikoku Island, which sandwich the Seto Inland Sea, and numerous industrial districts on the islands in the inland sea, are collectively called Setouch Industrial Region. Although its areal spread is large, the degree of industrial agglomeration is less than in Keihin and Hanshin.

In total industrial production by value, Sanyo, the north side of the Seto Inland Sea (Okayama, Hiroshima, and Yamaguichi Prefectures) is overwhelmingly larger than the south (Shikoku) side (Kagawa and Ehime Prefectures). The iron and steel, chemicals, transport machinery and equipment, oil refining, and petro-chemical industries are vastly greater than others on the north side. The south side's share in the heavy and chemical industries has increased rapidly recently, but is still inferior to the three prefectures in Sanyo.

DEVELOPMENT OF INDUSTRY AND CHARACTERISTICS OF THE REGION

The Seto Inland Sea was a waterway for transporting rice and other products to Osaka in the Edo Era, and with the coming of the Meiji Era and modern industrialisation in Hanshin ceñtred on Osaka, its importance as a waterway was extended with the transport of coal and cement from Kyushu.

The areas around the Seto Inland Sea, favoured with good conditions for agriculture, produced a considerable range of agricultural products, and therefore small industries for processing these products had existed earlier. Cotton fabric, for instance was produced everywhere in this region from the raw cotton produced in the coastal areas. The tatami matting made of rushes produced in the south of Okayama Prefecture and the indigo dyeing of Tokushima are famous, and in Hiroshima manufacture of Japanese paper, wooden clogs, wooden boats and so on had developed as traditional industries. Salt was extracted from sea water. Setouchi in fact had the most prosperous manufacturing industry in Japan in the Edo Era.

Modern industries were established during World War II in various areas individually, but their mutual linkage was rather poor. The industries utilising underground resources, the cement industry using limestone in Onoda in Yamaguchi Prefecture, the chemical industry using coal in Ube in Yamaguchi Prefecture, and the copper refinery industry using the copper ore of Niihama in Ehime Prefecture, became famous. Among them Niihama developed as the base of Sumitomo Zaitbatsu. In the Edo Era, Sumitomo carried on copper refining in Osaka, but around 1690 it very successfully developed the Besshi Copper Mine in the south of Niihama. Besshi was the best endowed copper mine in Japan in those days, and Sumitomo accumulated capital by refining the ore produced there. Niihama was originally merely a small farming and fishing village, but as the refining and shipping of copper became active as the base of Sumitomo Zaibatsu it grew apace. Air pollution by the gases from the refining process grew continuously from the beginning of the Meiji Era and became very serious by the middle of that Era. Then Sumitomo had to move the refinery plant to Shisaka Island, an off-shore island in 1905. Efforts to solve the air pollution problem induced the chemical industry to develop in Niihama, and superphosphate factories – which treated the sulphur dioxide gas from the refining process to produce fertiliser – and sulphuric acid factories were constructed. Ammonium, methanol, nitric acid and others were added from the later 1920s and these factories formed a comprehensive chemical industry. Sumitomo meantime expanded its business to include forests and coal for the copper mining and refining, machinery works, and copper wire drawing, and became a great Zaibatsu competing with Mitsubishi and Mitsui after World War I.

Among the industrial cities which developed by utilising underground resources, Ube and Onoda were different from Sumitomo in Niihama, and local influential businessmen provided the capital investment there. Ube as a chemical industrial city, based on submarine coal, is really a town of the Ube-Kosan Company, and the Onoda Cement Company, using the local limestone and coal from Ube, developed into the greatest cement maker in Japan.

However, in the Setouchi region, an agricultural area, no powerful industrial capital had been accumulated and the industries of the Seto Inland Sea region were developed by outside capital except for Ube, Onoda and Kurashiki, a Kurashiki Rayon Company town which developed from spinning to rayon manufacture. For example, the large-scale shipbuilding yards are those of large enterprises in Tokyo or Osaka, such as Mitsubishi, Mitsui, Hitachi, Kawasaki and Ishikawajima-Harima (IHI). In transport equipment, Toyo Kogyo, producing motor vehicles in Hiroshima, is managed by local capital, but locomotives, electric cars, freight cars, among others, are managed by Mitsubishi and Hitachi. In iron and steel there was only the factory of Nippon Steel Corporation in Himeji.

In the coastal areas of the Seto Inland Sea, chemical textile factories were located at various places from early in the Showa Era up to World War II. This reflected the gradual movement westward of the textile industry, with its heavy demand on water, from the Hanshin region, which had been the traditional centre of the industry.

The Seto Inland Sea region is a centre of the soda industry, which has a close relationship with salt manufacturing. As a special industry a naval arsenal in Kure in Hiroshima Prefecture produced war ships and steel materials until World War II.

Many single industrial towns were formed in the Seto Inland Sea region to take advantage of the mild and sunny climate, the relative freedom from typhoon damage, the ample labour supply in the coastal agricultural areas, and the sheltered sea for shipping. Most of the invested capital, however, belonged to large enterprises in Tokyo and Osaka.

DEVELOPMENT AFTER WORLD WAR II

Industrial development in the coastal areas of the Seto Inland Sea region advanced rapidly after World War II. In particular, with the expansion of Japanese industries in and after the 1960s, decentralisation of industry became mandatory because of the over-agglomeration in large industrial areas such as Keihin and Hanshin regions and the accompanying urban and pollution problems. At that time the Seto Inland Sea region was considered a desirable area for new industrial developments and as having superior locational conditions.

Three approaches were adopted in constructing the industrial sites. The first was the transfer of old military-use land after the end of the war. The facilities which had escaped war damage were converted for industrial use. The second was provided by rationalisation of the salt manufacturing process: the area of the salt-field was reduced, and the salt-fields were converted into industrial sites. The third was reclamation from the sea, which was undertaken on a large scale from around 1960. Ports accessible to large-size vessels, and extensive industrial land, were simultaneously provided by the reclamation. Almost all prefectures, cities and towns in the coastal areas made strenuous efforts to create industrial land in an attempt to improve the existing industrial structure by new growth industries.

Mizushima district in Okayama Prefecture made spectacular growth in the extensive development period of the 1960s. It had acquired a Mitsubishi factory for manufacturing military planes during the war. This factory was converted into a motor vehicle factory after the war, but the district was then designated as a New Industrial City; the harbour was dredged, much reclamation was done and a large industrial site was constructed. The first occupants were large-scale oil refining and petro-chemical factories of the Mitsubishi Group and an integrated steel plant of the Kawasaki Group. Currently 90 factories are located there. In Iwakuni in Yamaguchi Prefecture the Mitsui Group has a large-scale petro-chemical industrial complex, and in Tokuyama the Idemitsu Group has a similar one. Large-scale integrated steel plants are located in Fukuyama district in Hiroshima Prefecture, which adjoins Mizushima district.

The industries in the Seto Inland Sea region developed rapidly after World War II and there is some room for future

TABLE 19

Value of Industrial Shipments in the Setouchi Region, 1974

	* Sanyo		** North Shikoku	
	Value of Shipment (1,000 m. yen)	Percent	Value of Shipment (1,000 m. yen)	Percent
Total	9,802	100.0	2,701	100.0
Food and kindred products	728	7.3	264	9.7
Textiles	522	5.2	194	7.2
Lumber and wood products	442	4.4	155	5.7
Pulp, paper and allied products	225	2.2	263	9.7
Publishing, printing and allied industries	77	0.7	27	1.0
Chemicals and allied products	1,469	14.9	361	13.4
Petroleum and coal products	1,067	10.8	312	11.6
Ceramic, stone and clay products	467	4.7	73	2.7
Iron and steel	1,670	17.0	65	2.4
Non-ferrous metals and products	440	4.4	228	8.5
Fabricated metal products	303	3.0	87	3.2
Ordinary machinery	627	6.3	243	9.0
Electrical machinery, equipment and supplies	155	1.5	87	3.2
Transport equipment	1,459	14.8	247	9.2
Precision instruments	19	0.1	6	0.2
All other industries	269	2.7	89	3.3

* Prefectures of Okayama, Hiroshima and Yamaguchi (North side of the Seto Inland Sea)
** Prefectures of Kagawa and Ehime (South side of the Seto Inland Sea)

development, but the number of large-size vessels grew with the development of the industries, which increased the chances of accidents through traffic congestion. Environmental pollution also occurred. Air pollution by smoke and soot, sulphur oxides and so on, which became serious by the beginning of the 1960s, has been remarkably reduced by the development of new techniques, but no improvement has been made in the pollution of the inland sea. Fish were drastically reduced since they lost their egg-laying places with the reclamation of the shores and, further, the red tide, believed to be caused by the domestic and industrial effluent, occurs every summer, with great loss and damage to the fish breeding industry. Numerous islands scattered in the Seto Inland Sea contain many historical relics, and almost all of them are included in a national park. Industrial development in this region will have to be strictly controlled in the future.

Three bridges now under construction to join Honshu and Shikoku across the Seto Inland Sea, will improve conditions for the advancement of industry to the Pacific Coast of Shikoku Island. Control over the coastal areas of the Seto Inland Sea will be strengthened and at the same time the policy of attracting industries to the Pacific Coast of Shikoku Island will be made more positive in the future.

NORTHERN KYUSHU INDUSTRIAL REGION

The northern Kyushu Industrial Region generally means the area centred on Kita-Kyushu City,[1] which extends to the vicinity of Nakatsu City in Fukuoka Prefecture.

In addition, industrial cities such as Fukuoka City (Fukuoka Prefecture), Nagasaki City (Nagasaki Prefecture), Omuta City (Fukuoka Prefecture) in the coastal area of the Ariake Sea, Oita City (Oita Prefecture) on the east coast of Kyushu, and others, are distributed through the peripheral areas of Northern Kyushu. This is geographically the most western industrial region of the Japanese Islands, separated from Tokyo as the centre of Japan by approximately 1000 km. It is, however, near the Asian continent, particularly China and Korea.

The Northern Kyushu industrial region was once counted among the four major industrial regions in Japan, but its position declined gradually, as indicated in Chapter 1, and it is now considered one of the larger local industrial areas of Japan. Fukuoka Prefecture, centred on Kita-Kyushu City, accounts for 2.2% of the nationwide establishments, 3.0% of the workers and 1.7% of the shipment value. Iron and steel and food industries are very high in shipment value, and chemicals and machinery follow them. Northern Kyushu is an area where heavy and chemical industries specialise in iron and steel.

[1]Kita-Kyushu City, with a population of approximately one million was born by amalgamation of five industrial cities, Wakamatsu, Yawata, Tobata, Kokura and Moji, in 1963.

DEVELOPMENT OF MODERN INDUSTRY

The development of modern industries in this region was started by utilising underground resources, initially limestone. Although limestone was used as a fertiliser before the Meiji Era, its use as a raw material for cement was new. At first it was sent to Onoda in Yamaguichi Prefecture to be processed into cement, and cement factories were built successively in that area from 1892, making it an important industry.

Since production of cement is a simple process it did not cause any related industry to develop and did not play the role of a key industry for creating an industrial area, but it was significant in that it raised the value of coal as a basic resource in modern industry by providing coal with an industrial market at a time when it was used only for domestic fuel and salt manufacturing. It thereby promoted the development of coalfields in Northern Kyushu.

In Kyushu, Chikuho Coal Field, Miike Coal Field and various other large and small coalfields are distributed mostly in the western areas. The quality is comparatively good, bituminous coal occupying 70% of the total production

TABLE 20

Value of Industrial Shipments in the Northern Kyushu Industrial Region*

	Value of Shipment (1,000 mill. yen)	Per cent
Total	3,497	100.0
Food and kindred products	509	14.6
Textiles	83	2.4
Lumber and wood products	227	6.5
Pulp, paper and allied products	92	2.6
Publishing, printing and allied industries	105	3.0
Chemicals and allied products	310	8.9
Petroleum and coal products	58	1.7
Ceramic, stone and clay products	260	7.4
Iron and steel	800	22.9
Non-ferrous metals and products	123	3.5
Fabricated metal products	194	5.5
Ordinary machinery	302	8.6
Electrical machinery, equipment and supplies	161	4.6
Transport equipment	58	1.7
Precision instruments	3	—
All other industries	212	6.1

* Fukuoka Prefecture

quantity, but the coal seams are generally thin and the geological structure is complicated by folds and faults. Further, the coal lies deep, making mining even more difficult. However, like Hokkaido coal, it was important to Japan, which is short of coal resources.

Coalfields had been worked on a small scale since early times, and working was intensified in the Meiju Era. With the opening of the Chikuho Railway, development was continuously pushed forward by Zaibatsu such as Mitsui, Mitsubishi, Sumitomo and Furukawa. Initially coal was shipped across the Seto Inland Sea to Hanshin, but it became a base for a Northern Kyushu industrial region when a government ironworks was opened in Yahata in 1896. This establishing of a government ironworks in Yahata at that time determined the character of the Northern Kyusu industrial region for a long time. The first modern ironworks in Japan was the Kamaishi Ironworks in Iwate Prefecture, built to utilise local iron ore and charcoal. When smelting of iron ore by coke was introduced from overseas, a site for a new ironworks was widely sought in Keihin, Hanshin, Seto Inland Sea Coast and elsewhere. The choice fell on Western Japan: it was close to a coal-producing area, convenient for shipping and appropriate to the requirements of national defence. Yahata was the selected site.

No. 1 blast furnace started operating in 1901, iron ore being mainly supplied by the Tayeh Iron Ore Field of China. Since no modern industry at all had been developed in Northern Kyushu, the Yahata Iron Works had to adopt an integrated steel manufacturing system and equip related industrial sectors independently. The Russo-Japanese War of 1904–05 necessitated increased production of iron and steel which stimulated some development of related industries. Private enterprise established various metal-working and machinery undertakings to use the iron and steel, thereby forming an industrial area centering on the Yahata Ironworks. Private enterprise steel works were successively added to the government iron and steel works, and the outline of the present Northern Kyushu industrial region was almost complete at the time of World War I. The treatment of by-products from the coke ovens gave birth to the chemical industry. The Yahata

Ironworks also included a synthetic chemicals wing and produced, for example, ammonium, soda ash and plate glass. These chemical sectors are still important in the region.

The Northern Kyushu industrial region, where the weight of iron and steel and chemicals was already great, was further expanded and reinforced to tide over the depression following World War I. An arsenal was established in 1928, a drastic reorganisation was carried through in 1932, and the Yahata Ironworks changed to the Nippon Steel Corporation with only a 26% government holding. In 1937 Sumitomo constructed an open-hearth steel plant and in 1939 a blast furnace. The expansion of the heavy and chemical industries by the State and Zaibatsu made steady progress during the Sino-Japanese War and World War II, spurred by government and military demands, so that the region became one of the four major industrial areas in Japan. In this process the population of farming villages in southern Kyushu, where productivity was low, was rapidly absorbed by Northern Kyushu, where a group of industrial cities grew.

CHANGE AFTER WORLD WAR II

The Nippon Steel Corporation became a completely private enterprise after World War II, divided into Yahata and Fuji companies, thereby losing the protection of the state, which the Nippon Steel Corporation had enjoyed since the Meiji Era. The new companies also lost the Chinese sub-continent as the source of supply of raw materials and a market for the munitions industry. So the Northern Kyushu industrial region, whose major industry was iron and steel, encountered a critical turning point. In and after the 1960s Japanese industries made rapid progress, but the coal industry declined with the conversion to petroleum from coal as fuel. In particular, in Chikuho numerous medium and small coal mines closed in quick succession. Coal production fell rapidly. The numbers of unemployed increased. Coal miners, estimated at 70,000 persons in 1960, are now only 10% of that number.

Moreover, with the closing of mines, the management of the underground drifts and shafts was neglected, which brought about coal subsidence, accompanied by submersion of farming land under water and destruction of dwellings. As the problem has grown larger, the government has taken over the former coal collection sites and is giving assistance for introduction of new factories by various public investments. Since, however, the iron and steel industry is now oriented towards markets and not to raw materials because of the conversion to petroleum fuel and the development of new techniques in the industry and in transport, Northern Kyushu is no longer a superior location for the iron and steel industry. Some entrepreneurs are endeavouring to overcome the unfavourable locational conditions by rationalisation of factories, but some have left Kyushu and established new factories in Keihin or Hanshin regions.

Originally the Northern Kyushu region had a high ratio of production of basic material and most of its products were widely marketed raw in Japan. The metals and machinery industries, requiring high processing, therefore did not develop. At the time of the establishment of the Yahata Ironworks some of the local capital enterprises made considerable progress, but eventually they all came under the control of the great enterprises. The stagnation of basic industries in Northern Kyushu after the war obstructed the development of the medium and small subsidiary companies. As a result, the whole region was left behind in industrial development.

Northern Kyushu has other cities where industry is active. Consumer goods industries have developed in Fukuoka City, the central city of Kyushu, and Nagasaki City has long been famous for shipbuilding. Omuta City, which once had Miike coalfield and was Mitsui's base for the chemical industry, lost its activity through the conversion of raw material and fuel. Oita City, designated as a New Industrial City, has acquired an industrial complex of petroleum and iron and steel, built on land reclaimed from the sea.

Industrial development in the future, however, must avoid repeating the tragedy of the Minamata disease, a typical example of environmental damage in Kyushu. Minamata was a quiet fishing and salt extraction area facing the Shiranui Sea, but after the Chisso chemical works was located there, residents were ravaged by the effects of factory activities. The dusts of carbide and carbon invaded homes and also damaged agricultural products. The sea was polluted by waste water from factories, thereby gradually killing plankton, shell-fish and fish. Many of the residents who ate the marine products caught the disease, which in extreme cases destroyed the central nervous system and permanently disabled the victims. Not till after the 1960s was the cause of this disease identified and the victims helped, as mentioned in Part 6.

The super express train service from Tokyo has been extended to Hakata (Fukuoka City) through the Northern Kyushu industrial region. Airways also couple major cities in Kyushu and Tokyo. Kyushu is no longer remote as seen from Tokyo. This fact will help the future development of Northern Kyushu, but it will be equally important to facilitate close communication among the areas within Kyushu so that a really well-balanced economic development is realised. As long as an adequate rate of economic growth continues, Kyushu has sufficient room for accepting new industries.

2

Other Regions and Mill Towns

K. ITO AND I. OTA

(i) *THE HOKURIKU INDUSTRIAL REGION*

CHARACTERISTICS OF THE REGION

The Hokuriku region, extending along the Japan Sea in central Honshu, was already one of the powerful industrial regions in Japan before World War II. At present, too, industrial development has been realised in the highest level in the Japan Sea Belt. The value of industrial shipments in 1974 was 5 billion yen, 4.1% of the national production, and yet Hokuriku's share of the national industrial production has fallen below its pre-World War II level (Table 21). This declining tendency was most noticeable in the 1960s, Hokuriku having been left behind during the extensive development period.

TABLE 21

Manufacturing Industries in Hokuriku Region

Share of Hokuriku Region (per cent of value)	1930 4.9	1940 4.5	1965 4.0	1974 4.1
Total	100.0	100.0	100.0	100.0
Foods	9.2	5.3	7.4	7.0
Textiles	56.3	38.3	24.7	18.5
Lumber	2.0	2.4	5.0	6.0
Chemicals	25.1	21.4	24.0	15.2
Ceramics	1.3	1.4	3.1	4.3
Metals	1.7	15.1	16.1	16.6
Machinery	2.5	15.2	16.0	21.3
Others	2.1	1.2	3.7	3.3

Source: National Institute of Resource, Modernization and Location of Manufacturing Industries, 1957. MITI, Census of Manufacturers, 1965, 1974

Evidence for this 'left behind' position appears clearly in the type of industries, too: the major industries before World War

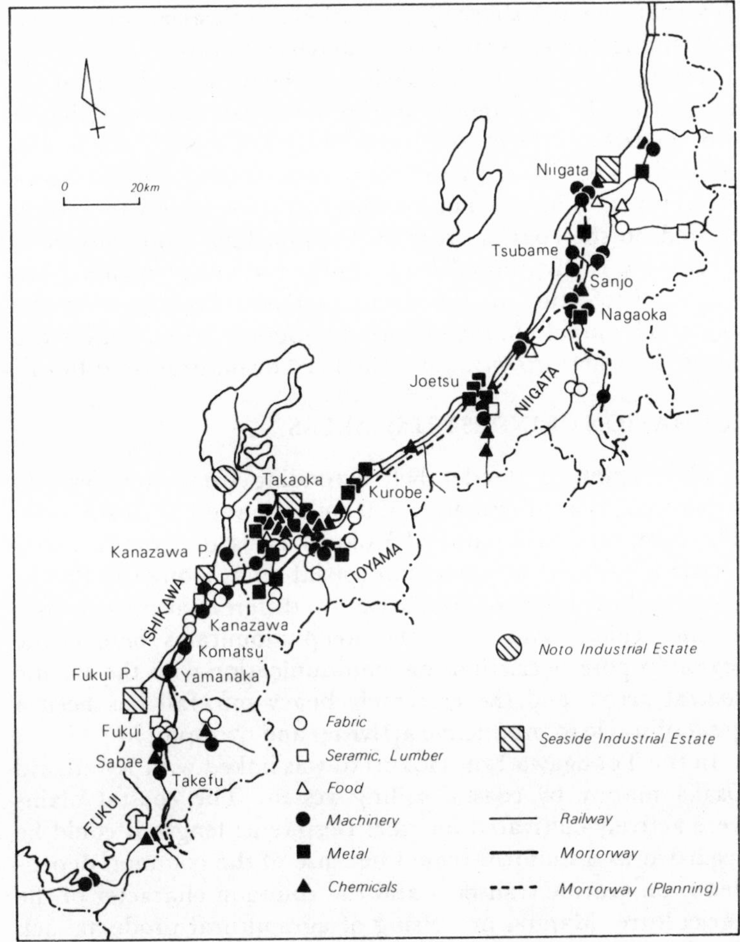

Fig. 3.1 Distribution of main factories (500 workers or more) in Hokuriku region

II, such as textiles, iron and steel, chemicals and machinery, still compose the major industries in this region.

True, new industries, including electrical machinery, non-ferrous metals and others, have developed in recent years, and the industrial structure shows change (Table 21). The growth of the machinery and metal industries, however, has not offset the decline of the textile and chemical industries, so the

Hokuriku region's share of the national industrial production is declining and the structural weakness remains.

Among these major industries the heavy and chemical industries are located mostly in the north-east district (Niigata and Toyama Prefectures), and the textile and machinery industries are strong in the south-west (Fukui and Ishikawa Prefectures). The new non-ferrous metal industries are mostly located on the coastal areas of Toyama Bay, while electrical machinery is distributed over almost the entire region from Niigata Prefecture in the north to Fukui Prefecture in the south. The areal characteristics mentioned earlier reflect the industries whose growth was influenced by natural conditions.

FORMATION OF INDUSTRIAL AREAS

This region, a slender belt extending from north-east to south-west, is approximately 500 km long and 60–70 km wide. The comprehensive name of Hokuriku obscures the fact that relations with the advanced industrial areas along the Pacific Coast and the metropolitan areas are different at the two ends of the region. Moreover, the steep mountains behind the region impose restrictions on communication with the Pacific coastal areas, and the extremely heavy snowfall has been a great obstacle to productive activities and transport.

In the Tokugawa Era, Hokuriku was linked with Kyoto and Osaka mainly by coastal sailing vessels. The coastal plains were actively cultivated for rice. Despite its length it could be regarded as a uniform region because of the common dependence on marine transport and the common character of the agriculture. Manual processing of agricultural products such as silk-reeling and weaving, timber processing, some industries (lacquerware, for example), and manufacture of agricultural tools developed early, using traditional techniques. Areas of specialised production arose after the Meiji Restoration and still exist: fabrics (Fukui Prefecture, Ishikawa Prefecture, the plains part of Niigata Prefecture); lacquer wares (Wajima, Yamanaka of Ishikawa Prefecture); medicine manufacturing (Toyama City and its surroundings); table wares (Tsubame in Niigata Prefecture); cutlery (Sanjo in Niigata Prefecture, Takeo in Fukui Prefecture); and spectacle frames (Sabae in Fukui Prefecture).

However, the uniformity that was evident in the Edo Period gradually declined from the beginning of the 20th century, following the transfer of the Metropolis to Tokyo after the Meiji Restoration and the construction of railway networks centering on Tokyo and Osaka. The north-east district of Hokuriku (Niigata and Toyama Prefectures), being close to Kanto, rapidly strengthened its relation with Tokyo, while the south-west district (Fukui and Ishikawa Prefectures) still maintained a strong relationship with Kyoto and Osaka. The gap between these two districts was a powerful influence on the industrial development of Hokuriku thereafter.

THE NORTH-EAST DISTRICT

This district is backed by a zone of steep mountains where snow accumulates heavily in winter and has favoured hydro-electric power development along the rivers. The first power station, a small one, was constructed by an electric light company in Toyama in 1899, but after about 1910 hydro-electric power development in Japan generally made considerable advances and gradually progressed in this district. At first, however, demand was much below supply and the cheapness of the surplus electric power encouraged the location in the district of many electrical smelting and electro-chemical works from about 1930. They belonged mainly to companies with head offices in Tokyo and it was the growth of these power-oriented industries linked with power-source development that characterised the industries of the north-east district before World War II.

Even after World War II these electrolysis and electric furnace industries continued to be the main industries, until the 1960s. The post-war power policy, however, almost killed the locational advantage of cheap surplus electric power in Hokuriku and, further, the post-war technological revolution made these industries obsolescent. Their continued development, therefore, cannot be anticipated. Although the chemical industry was established before and after 1960 in the vicinity of Niigata City to utilise the plentiful natural gas in the lower courses of the River Shinano and the River Agano, its development was restricted, since the pumping up of underground water accompanying exploitation of natural gas brought about rapid ground subsidence.

In order to stop this decline of industries, two new industrial cities, Toyama–Takaoka and Niigata, based on the Comprehensive National Development Plan, were set up. These two plans, implemented from 1969, each aimed at excavating a large scale port and constructing a coastal industrial area to provide a suitable location for the most advanced and large-scale heavy and chemical industries as major industries and improve the regional economy. Sumitomo's aluminium refinery was located in the Toyama–Takaoka district in 1973, and related processing plants were built. In consequence this area bids fair to become an important centre of the Japanese aluminium industry.

In Niigata, too, introduction of metal, machinery, chemical, electric power and lumber industries is planned, and not a few factories have already started operation. As the aluminium industry in Toyama–Takaoka clearly shows, however, the industries in the north-east district are still heavy consumers of electricity, and this presages a serious problem of supply of electric power in the future.

THE SOUTH-WEST DISTRICT

Weaving was an ancient rural industry in various places here, and about the end of the 19th century production of highest quality silk fabrics, Habutae, was started for export. Its success was the basis for the development of the fibre industry, centering on the weaving industry, to its present nature and importance. Power looms began to replace the traditional hand looms in 1910. When the export of Habutae silk declined in World War I, the production of staple-fibre fabrics was undertaken and this district became the largest Japanese producing centre of staple-fibre fabrics for export around 1930. Accompanying this conversion from silk to staple-fibre fabrics, relations with fabric Toiya and trading firms in Osaka became closer, thus widening the difference from the north-east district, whose close relations are with Tokyo.

After World War II, when synthetic fibre was developed, the staple-fibre fabrics centre of Hokuriku region was reorganised as a synthetic fabrics centre by major synthetic fibre companies and fabric commission agents. The weaving industrialists in this district specialise in producing extremely thin cloth, in part an inheritance from the earlier production of Habutae silk, and now occupy a monopolistic position in Japan for high class thin synthetic fabrics. Most of their production is exported, principally to the United States.

Generally speaking, a few major synthetic fabric makers put their weaving industrialists into their own systematised control, directly or through fabric commission agents, and therefore almost all of the weaving industrialists in Hokuriku have become sub-contracted companies of these major synthetic fabric makers. The textile industry in this region developed originally to take advantage of all-year-round high humidity and cheap female labour in the farming villages, and there are still many small-scale domestic factories where family members also work long hours at home in addition to farming.

Prospects for the fabric industry in Hokuriku, however, are not without anxieties, because of chronic over-production and the catching-up of developing countries. Consequently, efforts are being made to convert the industry into a more competitive, highly processed, and more promising and stabilised industrial structure, such as advancing into the clothing manufacturing industry.

Closely related with the development of the textile industry of the south-west district is the textile machinery industry, centred on Kanazawa City. Kanazawa City in the Tokugawa Era was the largest city after Edo (Tokyo), Osaka and Kyoto and the castle town of the Kaga clan, which was the greatest clan represented by a lord. Many types of handwork industries had been developed, and among them gold lacquer, Kyoto-type dye, gilding and others, still exist as traditional industries and lend colour to Hokuriku industry. On the other hand, in addition to the techniques and capital accumulated in the modern age, the production of Habutae silk for export gave a stimulus to the production of weaving machines. The first weaving machine factory was established in 1883 and the number of factories increased gradually after 1900. As the Hokuriku textile industry changed from silk to staple-fibre and from staple-fibre to synthetic fabrics, the weaving machinery industry developed correspondingly to form a characteristic textile machine producing centre specialising in silk and staple-fibre looms. The textile machinery industry was developed by local capital and its further development is expected to be into diversification. The textile industry, however, is suffering from structural stagnation and the prospect for its conversion into a growth industry is poor.

To break this stagnation of industry in the south-west district, construction of a new port and preparation of coastal industrial areas are going forward, following the example of the north-east district in Ishikawa and Fukui Prefectures. The development of the district as an industrial area of a new character is difficult, however, in view of the relationship with existing industries and geographical conditions. No progress has been made in attracting new heavy and chemical industries.

NEW INDUSTRIES AND RECENT TRENDS

Apart from the character imported to the Hokuriku region by the two differing districts, there are three characteristic manufacturing companies worthy of mention. These are the Komatsu Engineering KK, the Niigata Engineering Company and the Yoshida Kogyo KK. Komatsu Engineering was established in Komatsu City in Ishikawa Prefecture in 1919 as a repair works for copper mining machinery. It produced tanks during World War II, and finally became a company representing Hokuriku as a maker of fork lifts and bulldozers. Niigata Engineering was established in 1909 to produce and repair machinery for oil field development, but has diversified into ships, vehicles, machine tools, and diesel engines, among others. Yoshida Kogyo, known by its trade mark, YKK, moved its main works from Tokyo to Kurobe City in Toyama Prefecture during World War II and has become the largest zip-fastener maker in the world. Yoshida Kogyo now has many factories in foreign countries and has adopted a unique system of integrated production: all raw materials, such as aluminium, cotton cloth and plastics, are domestically produced in the main factory. Refined aluminium is used as material not only for fasteners but also for window sashes, of which also it is the biggest Japanese producer.

New development became noticeable about 1965, while old industries declined and were left behind. Knitting and electronics appliance industries in large central cities used to operate by collecting female operatives from provincial areas, but competition for labour accompanying the new developments obliged them, as labour-intensive industries, to disperse to Hokuriku region to secure labour. Wages, however, are low compared with those of advanced areas and the spread effect on the regional economy is small. Industrial development is somewhat tardy in Hokuriku.

(ii) *SINGLE INDUSTRY MILL TOWNS*

FORMATION OF MILL TOWNS

There are industrial cities outside any large industrial region whose industrial character is determined by specific enterprises in a single industrial field. Some are cities which have newly developed from purely rural areas and in others industries were located in existing cities. Later some may find themselves included in a large city area or conurbation. It is becoming increasingly difficult for a mill town to remain simply a mill town, but Toyota, now included in the large metropolitan area of Nagoya, and Yahata, now part of Kita-Kyushu City, still maintain the character of mill towns or communities of a single industry. Toyota is the Toyota Motor Corporation town and Kita-Kyushu is still an iron manufacturing industrial city.

There are three phases in the formation of mill towns or company towns where the industry of a specific company is predominant. The first is represented by cities industrially oriented to material, such as Yahata, Kamaishi and Muroran in the iron and steel industry and Tomakomai in paper manufacturing, which were established early in the present century. Yahata, whose local coal attracted iron mills, was consolidated with four neighbouring cities and became Kita-Kyushu City in 1963. The new city as a whole is no longer simply an iron town, but iron and steel products are still the leading output.

Muroran and Kamaishi have always been isolated steel centres. In particular, Kamaishi is in a locality too isolated for other industries to develop, and is a typical mill town, where more than 70% of the municipal economy is supported by Nippon Steel. Tomakomai has been planning transformation into a new heavy and chemical industrial city since 1964 but is still essentially an Oji Paper Company town.

The second phase extends from World War I to the 1930s. Cities dominated by the heavy and chemical industries, heavy consumers of electric power, the electrical machinery industry, with copper products as raw material and linked with refineries or copper mines, and their related industries, characterised this phase. The nationwide development of electric power in this period stimulated development of both industries. This was also a period when new Zaibatsu were added to old Zaibatsu. For instance, Kuhara Zaibatsu, which managed a copper mine in Hitachi in Northern Kanto, established electrical machinery works in its local area and changed a small village to a large mill town. In Kyushu, Noguchi Zaibatsu constructed factories for chemical fertilisers, fibres, medicines and powder in Nobeoka in Miyazaki Prefecture powered by hydro-electricity and laid the basis of today's industrial town of Asahi Kasei. Among the old Zaibatsu, too, Sumitomo installed machinery and chemical works at Niihama near the Besshi copper mine in Shikoku, and Mitsui Zaibatsu developed coal and chemical industries in Omuta to utilise the coal at Miike in Kyushu. In addition, electricity-oriented chemical works and metal refineries spread widely to numerous other towns, but these are not mill towns or company towns. These Hokuriku industries developed rapidly in this period.

The third stage is the period of rapid economic growth after World War II. The iron and steel industry occupied the central position in the new industrial cities, but oil refining and the petro-chemical industry joined it.

In contrast to pre-war days very few industries were attracted by natural resources and/or motive power: virtually all were port- or market-oriented type industries. Few of the mill towns formed in this period are remote from a large city area or a large industrial region. Any town acquiring an iron and steel industry is likely to approximate to a single industry mill town, since this industry has a powerful integration process and heavy demand for labour. An oil refinery or petrochemical works seldom initiates a single-company town, since these industries do not require a large labour force, and plural enterprise groups are normally characteristic. Examples are Kashima and Kamisu in Ibaraki Prefecture (Sumitomo-Mitsubishi group) near Tokyo, Ichihara and Goi of Chiba Prefecture (a multi-enterprise group) and Kimitsu (Nippon Steel), also in Chiba Prefecture. These towns or cities are instances of agricultural or fishing villages changing with dramatic rapidity into industrial cities, as are Tokai in south Nagoya (Nippon Steel) and Mizushima of Okayama Prefecture (Kawasaki Steel and Mitsubishi group). Outside the company towns, existing cities such as Yokkaichi, Iwakuni and Otake made progress in this period as industrial cities.

MURORAN CITY

Muroran City has the largest industrial output by value in Hokkaido. About half the production is accounted for by the iron and steel industry, and with the related machine industry, the total share reaches 70%. Two large mills have produced iron and steel products supported by military demands since 1906. Since the factories were constructed in a lonely and isolated village, workers' houses had to be built, and when the two factories entered full operation in 1915, 50 households of the pre-industrial village had become 7,400 households, holding a population of 35,000. Iron and steel industry workers then numbered some 8,000, who with their dependants meant that more than 80% of the total population were dependent upon the company and the village had become an iron town. The company provided all necessary residential facilities. It held the water rights on the major local rivers to supply its own water for industrial use and its employees' water for domestic use. Beyond that water was sold to the town-managed water supply system, and it was not until 1928 that Muroran Town succeeded in securing the independence of its water supply system from the company. Such control of water rights by industry is not uncommon in Japan, and Muroran affords a typical example. The main reason for the company's selection of this location for the iron and steel industry was its proximity to the producing centres of iron ore and coal, but with today's dependence upon imported raw materials it is the port facilities that are crucial and they make Muroran the most important heavy industrial centre in Hokkaido.

HITACHI CITY

This is one of the leading industrial cities in East Japan. North of Hitachi City there is no industrial city comparable with it, and in the great Tokyo Metropolitan area in the south, only six industrial cities are larger than Hitachi. An auxiliary machinery repair department was started at the copper mine in 1907, and this department separated and became independent as Hitachi Engineering, which stimulated the growth of an electrical machinery manufacturing town. Since the local agricultural villages could not supply sufficient labour suitable for modern industry, most of the workers were recruited from outside Ibaraki Prefecture. Because of the contemporaneous power revolution, generators and power-feeding machines produced by this company had a wide market, and the village, population 6,000 in 1907, rapidly grew to a medium-size city with a population of 70,000 in 1938. The factories and employees' houses presented a conspicuous landscape in Hitachi City. As usual with company towns in Japan, since the company provided exclusive use houses and retail stores for the employees, the city's own functions did not grow on the same scale as the population. Hitachi Engineering itself managed supply of the power, water and city gas systems. The company also controlled real estate business and not only the major industries but also virtually all other industries, and Hitachi literally became a town of a single enterprise. This monopolistic and diversified management was possible because it originated in an undeveloped rural area, void of any competing enterprise. When the main factory was reconstructed and the centre of the housing area removed to a new location, the old business centre of the city declined and a new business street was born near the housing area – a good demonstration of the influencing power of Hitachi Engineering. Its employees had little contact with the old community, the services provided by the enterprise catering for most of their daily requirements.

NOBEOKA CITY

This is a chemical industry city where the Asahi Chemicals group of factories demonstrates its grand design. The industrial production value is not particularly large from the national viewpoint, but it is unique in South Kyushu, where industrialisation was tardy. After Noguchi Zaibatsu opened a synthetic ammonia processing plant in 1923, the quiet castle town began to be surrounded by factories. When the import of chemical products from Europe was halted by World War I and a real chemical industry was beginning to develop in Japan, the formerly stagnant local central city was actively seeking modern industries. The villages surrounding the old Nobeoka town all took positive measures to attract factories. They competed in furnishing land for industrial use. When the factories were constructed, dispersed in three villages, the company demanded organisation of a new autonomous public authority for the three villages to obtain common regulations for plant operation, and the local authorities accepted this demand. In 1950 the company caused the three villages to be amalgamated with the old Nobeoka City. This kind of reorganisation of administrative sections following demands by the industrialists has occurred in various places in Japan since early in this century. In Nobeoka, where the enterprise has all the greater weight since the city is small, the influencing power of Asahi Chemicals in the city administration is extremely strong. There have been instances where both the management and the labour union of the company recommended candidates in the election of mayor or members of the municipal assembly and they were elected. Local administration could not be carried on if the requirements of Asahi Chemicals, which is the greatest tax income source of the city, were disregarded.

Problems of environmental pollution, which inevitably accompany development of the chemical industry, were pointed out by fishermen in the later 1920s. The company conducted repeated negotiations with the fishermen and farmers, but techniques for measuring the extent of pollution were inadequate and neither the enterprise, the administration nor the residents had any definite knowledge or opinion concerning environmental problems. So no fundamental solution was found. Meantime the Asahi Chemicals employees showed no serious concern for the fishermen and farmers. The employees who had come from other areas as industrial workers had little interest in the old residents whose way of living was quite different from theirs. The fact that many farmers and fishermen had relatives in Asahi Chemicals employment added another dimension to the difficulty of coping effectively with the pollution problem.

In fact, in any area residents of a mill town can hardly criticise the enterprise which increases the chances of employment of local residents and pays a high amount of municipal taxes. In other words, in an industrial city whether it is controlled by a single enterprise or whether plural enterprises are specialised in a specific industry, it is difficult to activate the efforts of local residents to solve environmental problems.

PART FOUR

Development and Distribution of the Main Manufacturing Industries – 1

1

Textiles

H. NAITO

POSITION AND CHARACTERISTICS

DEVELOPMENT AND POSITION

The textile industry played a leading role in the capitalistic industrialisation of Japan during and after the Meiji Era. Its prime period of prosperity was before and after 1930, when raw cotton consumption was second only to that of the United States and cotton cloth exports led the world, having surpassed the British. Thus, Japan occupied an important position in the textile market of the world.

The textile industry provided about 50% of total industrial production throughout the Meiji and Taisho Eras and about 40% around 1930. From the Meiji Era to about 1930 50–60% of the total industrial workers were engaged in the textile industry and textile products reached 57% of total exports (1934–6 average). The Japanese economy till then was characterised by an industrial structure of predominantly light industries, centring on the textile industry.

World War II dealt a serious blow to the Japanese textile industry: development was drastically curtailed under the policy of giving priority to heavy industries for the war economy, and, further, it sustained direct war damage. The developing countries in Asia, Africa and Latin America, too, adopted policies for industrialisation, especially for promotion of light industries, particularly the textile industry. In consequence the export markets of the Japanese textile industry were narrowed. The developing countries, thanks to low wages, produced cheap products, precisely as pre-war Japan had done, and became powerful competitors to advanced countries, including Japan.

From 1955, the heavy and chemical industries made great strides under the extensive development policy and the position of the textile industry fell rapidly. It gradually became a backward industrial sector, a labour-intensive light industrial sector where the value added is low. The percentage of the output of textile products to total industrial output fell rapidly after its peak of 25% in 1951. By 1955 it was 17.5%, by 1960, 12.4%, by 1970, 7.8%. and by 1975, only 6.8%. Along with this continuous decline, however, synthetic fibre was rapidly replacing natural fibre, and the synthetic textile industry was booming. The natural textile industry was affected by chronic over-production, and in and after the 1960s new or expanded installations were restricted in both spinning and weaving. Furthermore, government policy is encouraging destruction of excess equipment, closure of factories or transfer to another business.

STRUCTURE AND CHARACTERISTICS

The structure of the textile industry varies. The classification in the Census of Manufacturers divides it into three sectors; the fibre industry, the fibre products manufacturing industry and the synthetic fibre manufacturing industry in the chemical industry, and in a more detailed classification increases the number of sectors to 16.

Classified by processing, the industry includes the following processes:

1. The primary processing stage – silk reeling, spinning and synthetic fibre production.
2. The secondary processing stage – weaving, knitting, lace-making, for example.
3. The tertiary processing stage – clothing industry (chiefly the sewing industry).

So there are many stages from the original yarn to the final products, and the social division of labour applies as in other industries. In other words, the development of the enterprise, the degree of capital accumulation and the technical level are different in different sectors. Each sector has horizontal specialisation and no enterprise has a vertically integrated processing system. If the textile industry is compared with the flow of a river, the primary processing stage is the upper reaches, the secondary processing stage the middle reaches, and the tertiary processing stage the lower reaches, and the textile industry as a whole reveals a vertical structure.

In 1970 textile factories numbered 157,381, of which the raw yarn sector accounted for 1772, the secondary sector 68,184 and the third sector 61,179. The first and the final stages contrast strikingly in the scale of factory and in labour productivity. The primary processing sector, producing yarns, is generally large-scale and has high productivity. In cotton spinning, ten major companies form the core of production, accounting for 55% of total spinning equipment, and production is concentrated even further in fewer enterprises in the synthetic fibre industry.

In the weaving, knitting and clothing industries, on the other hand, the scale of factories is small and productivity is low. Workers per factory number 824 in the synthetic fibre industry and 129 in the spinning industry, but only 5 in the weaving industry, 11 in the knitting industry and 12 in the clothing industry. (1975). In addition, there are numerous extremely small production units which escape statistical enumeration, such as handloom-weaving in the farming villages or as domestic side employment in the urban areas. This kind of dual structure in the textile industry resulted from the fact that influential spinning companies, synthetic fibre companies and influential Toiya used their financial, planning and technical power to systematise the weaving, knitting and sewing sectors. The small-scale weaving and knitting industries are frequently concentrated in specific areas, together with related industries, seeking the advantages of agglomeration and usually distributors such as brokers, wholesalers and so on also congregate in the areas where production is concentrated.

In addition to the social division of labour characteristic of the textile industry, individual companies and dealers are connected by the sub-contract system which establishes the relationship between the controller and the controlled, and this relationship is seen between areas as well as between enterprises. For instance, the weaving industry in Tango district in the north of Kyoto Prefecture developed this district as a sub-contract area of the Nishijin silk weaving industry of Kyoto City.

The sub-contract system exists not only in the production sector but also between the producers and Toiya and the commercial firms. The controlling power of Toiya declined generally after the war but is still strong in the clothing and knitting industries.

Thus, as mentioned above, the organisation of textile production is complex, with a characteristic dual structure.

We shall now examine the structural change of the textile industry. Among textile-related industries the number of workers drastically declined in 1960–74 in the spinning and the weaving industries. In contrast the rapid increase in the number of workers in the knitting and the clothing industries cancelled out that decrease and so the index of workers' numbers in the industry as a whole remained at 1.02. Since the increase in the total number of workers in Japanese industry was 1.41 times in this period, the position of the textile industry had declined drastically. The growth of the knitting industry and the clothing industry was based on the increase of fashionable consumption in the economic growth period and on favourable export conditions. The clothing sector is confidently expected to be a pacemaker in any revival of the textile industry.

DISTRIBUTION OF INDUSTRY

THE PRIMARY PROCESSING SECTOR (RAW YARN)

(a) Silk reeling. Silk reeling from domestic cocoons is an ancient industry. It was, consequently, along with tea, an important export product in the early stages of the Meiji Era, and domestic and overseas demands supported steady development thereafter. Silkworm-raising replaced cotton cultivation as an important cash income source for farming households, and the mulberry-growing areas, centred on such central prefectures as Nagano, Gumma, Fukushima, expanded remarkably. Silk reeling factories were established successively, mainly in those silkworm-raising zones, but competition from synthetic fibre (particularly nylon) and, after World War II, from cheap Chinese raw silk, hit silk reeling and silkworm-

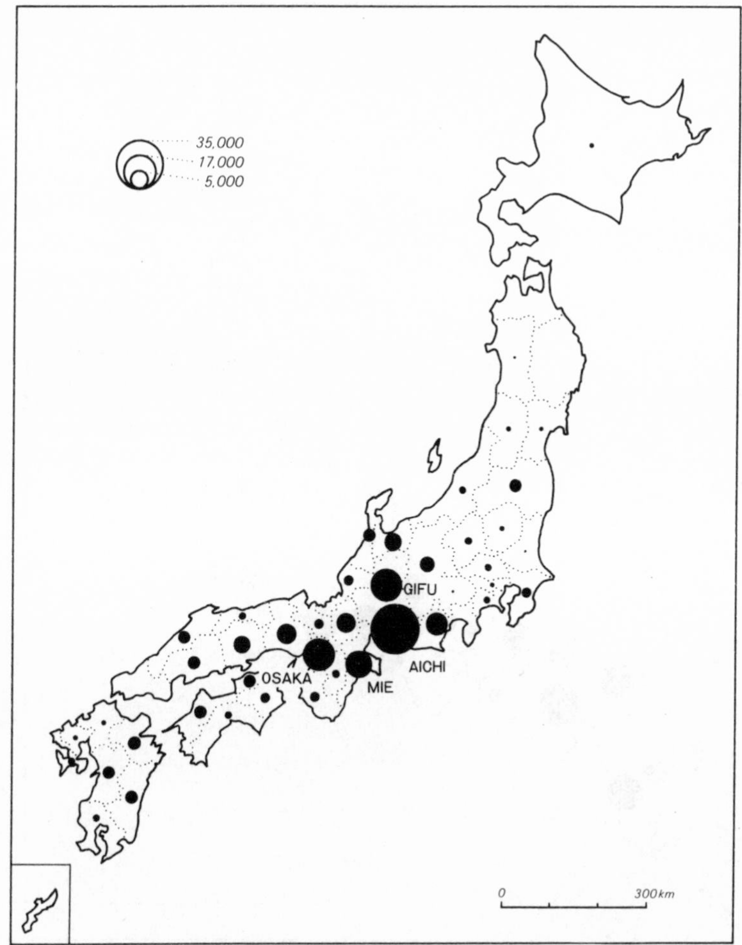

Fig. 4.1 Distribution of spinning industry by number of workers, 1974

raising hard. The mulberry-growing area declined progressively from its peak in the mid-1920s and silk reeling has also declined drastically.

In 1975 silk reeling factories numbered 1206, 84% of them having fewer than 100 workers. They are widely distributed in central Japan, in the areas of the silkworm-raising industry, which are essentially limited to the uplands. Nagano Pre-

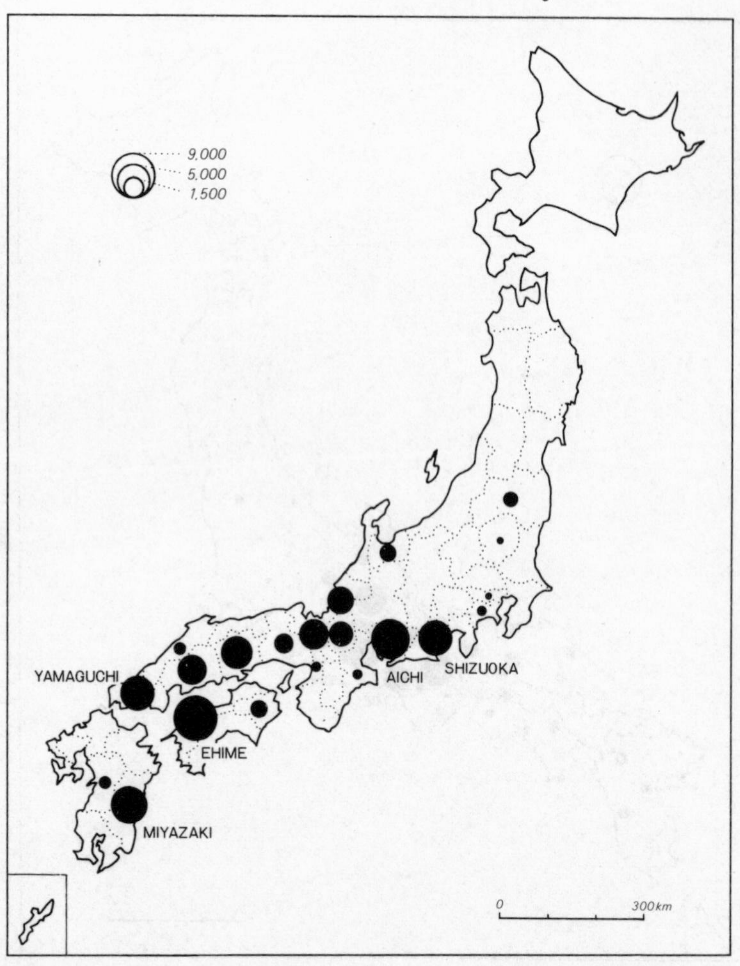

Fig. 4.2 Distribution of chemical fibre industry by number of workers, 1974

fecture leads in the number of silk reeling establishments.

(b) Cotton spinning. Cotton spinning centres on Tokai and Hanshin regions, both regions formerly centres of cotton cultivation. Government spinning factories were established in cotton-cultivating areas early in the Meiji Era, and the distribution of cotton spinning today reflects that early start. With importing of cheaper raw cotton from overseas, cotton

cultivation declined but Yokkaichi and Nagoya were advantageously located and well equipped as specialist cotton importing ports and Kobe as a general trading port, so that Tokai and Hanshin regions were still favoured for access to raw materials. In cotton-cultivating areas, cotton spinning had developed and the location of spinning factories promoted the development of the weaving industry, which in turn reinforced the cotton spinning industry. With this mutual support Tokai and Hanshin grew in strength as cotton spinning and weaving regions.

In contrast to the wide distribution of cotton spinning in south-west Japan, wool spinning is concentrated into four prefectures, Aichi, Gifu, Mie and Osaka, and its distribution is more restricted in area.

(c) Synthetic Fibre. This industry is subject to location conditions different from those of natural fibre industries. More weight is attached to the availability of a large supply of high quality water, to good transport conditions for the raw materials and to large supplies of electric power rather than to accessibility to textile-producing areas or to its market. As a result, synthetic fibre industry factories were located in various places in south-western Japan, centring on the Seto Inland Sea. After World War II, however, the improvement in transport of raw materials and recycling of industrial water, favoured the influence of markets and therefore of Hanshin and Tokai regions. Synthetic fibres is a new industrial sector, which developed after the war, using raw materials from the petrochemical industry. The factories, therefore, are located to link with petro-chemical complexes.

As mentioned, the distribution of the primary processing sector corresponds pretty well with the distribution of the traditional cotton spinning, wool spinning and silk reeling. Cotton spinning and synthetic fibre are located in the Pacific Coastal Belt from Tokai to Setouchi, while silk reeling supplements cotton spinning from central Japan to southern Tohuku. Wool spinning occupies some of the cotton spinning area in the Hanshin and Tokai regions. Accordingly, the location of the primary processing sector as a whole conforms to the location of the raw material and processing sector, except for the new locational trend of the synthetic fibre industry.

THE SECOND AND THIRD PROCESSING SECTORS

(a) Weaving. The weaving industry is a representative traditional Japanese industry, and the textile-producing areas that were formed before the Meiji Era were the precursors of today's textile producing areas. Urban industries such as the Nishijin silk of Kyoto which developed to fill the demands of the nobility were exceptional; most of the traditional producing areas were based on farm village industries. Tokai, Hanshin, and Hokuriku (Fukui and Ishikawa Prefectures) are large producing areas. Of these Tokai region is characterised by cotton and wool, Hanshin by cotton, Kyoto by silk and synthetic textiles and Hokuriku by synthetic textiles. The main product of these great producing areas, except Kyoto, is cloth for Western-style suits, but various medium and small areas as well as Kyoto produce cloth for Japanese kimonos.

In the rapid economic growth period after World War II industrial weaving increased remarkably in the farming areas in Hokuriku region and Kyoto Prefecture, while weaving industrialists increasingly closed or transferred their urban establishments. These opposite trends resulted from the respective circumstances of the farming villages and the urban areas. Firstly, farming households, because of the decline of agriculture, needed to supplement their agricultural income. Weaving, which could be started with small funds, met this requirement. Secondly, the weaving industry with its low productivity and low wage level had to compete in the urban areas with other industries, and the situation was worsened by rising wage levels. Thirdly, the synthetic fibre makers and their related commercial firms took the initiative in promoting the weaving industry in agricultural areas, where labour was available at low wages. So weaving mills increased in the farming areas and decreased in the urban areas. This tendency characterised the whole country in the economic growth period, although there were differences in degree.

(b) Knitting. The knitting industry was imported after the Meiji Era and developed in large cities such as Tokyo, Osaka and Nagoya. It made particularly rapid progress after World War II and has spread through the whole country. Producing areas of the knitting industry may be classified into (1) those which were located in cheap labour areas – in large cities such

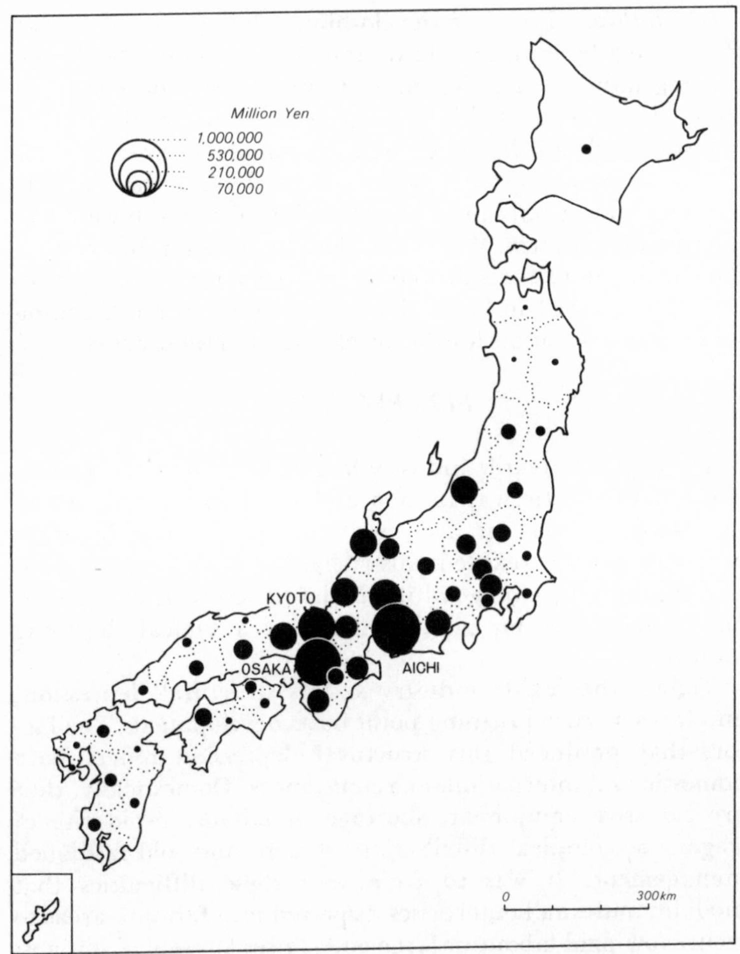

Fig. 4.3 Distribution of yarn and fabric industry by shipment, 1974

as Tokyo and Osaka, (2) those which were located in farming villages surrounding urban areas, and (3) those which were located in traditional cotton and silk textile producing areas and silk reeling areas, where the business was converted into production of knitted goods. The increase in factory numbers was particularly remarkable in farming areas, and especially in silkworm-raising and silk reeling areas, where supplementary work was provided for farming households.

(c) Clothing. Trends in the clothing industry, the final stage of the textile industry, have much in common with the knitting industry. Firstly, the clothing industry developed in large cities; secondly, it is a growth sector in the textile industry; and, thirdly, its growth was mainly in farming areas in the economic growth period. Therefore, it has a wide distribution not only in urban areas but also nationwide like the knitting industry. Where the clothing industry differs from the knitting industry is that comparatively large-scale factories originally located in large cities were dispersed into farming areas, which accounts for the development of these areas.

PERSPECTIVE

The Japanese textile industry largely depended on exports. This characteristic was formed and has been maintained in the whole process of the modernisation of the Japanese economy, but the textile industry has lost its old central position through the change of industrial structure after the war, and is now showing all the marks of a typical declining industry.

Today, the textile industry suffers structural depression, and faces a crucial turning point in its development. The factors that produced this structural depression reflect both domestic and international circumstances. Domestically, they are excessive equipment, shortage of labour, rapid rise of wages, a complex distribution system and old-fashioned management. It was to cope with these difficulties that medium and small enterprises dispersed into farming areas to secure low-paid labour or large enterprises attempted business reorganisation by amalgamation or take-over of enterprises and by rationalisation and modernisation of equipment.

Internationally the competitive power of the Japanese textile industry has fallen. In particular, since the war, developing countries relying on cheap labour, have developed their textile industries remarkably, and former importing countries have become self-supporting or export countries. The cotton yarn, cotton and staple fibre textiles of Japan have almost completely lost their competitive power in exports through the development of textile industries in, for example,

Korea, Hong Kong, Taiwan, India and Pakistan.

The Japanese textile industry faces many difficulties. A way must be found for survival in a sector which has high productivity of value added.

2

Energy

T. YADA

OUTLOOK

In Japan, energy remained dependent upon domestic water power and coal for half a century after the establishment of modern industry up to about the mid-1950s, thus maintaining a high degree of self-sufficiency for a surprisingly long time. Even in 1955, ten years after the end of World War II, the supply of primary energy was 44.8% from domestic coal and 21.2% from water power generation. The total of domestically provided energy was 76.0%. The situation changed, however, with the arrival of 'low price crude oil' from the Middle East. The wave of 'the energy revolution' which had already attacked western European countries attacked Japan overwhelmingly from the later 1950s.

TABLE 22

Composition Ratio of Supply of Primary Energy (Fiscal year)

	1955		1975	
	10^{10} cal.	%	10^{10} cal.	%
Water power	11,883	21.2	21,047	5.8
Atomic power	—		6,156	1.7
Coal	28,135	50.2	60,250	16.4
Domestic	25,670	45.8	12,212	3.3
Imported	2,465	4.4	47,945	13.3
Petroleum	11,301	20.2	268,812	73.3
Domestic	335	0.6	656	0.2
Imported	10,966	19.6	268,156	73.1
Natural gas, LNG	238	0.4	9,391	2.5
Charcoal, woods	4,459	8.0	983	0.3
Total	56,016	100.0	366,641	100.0
Domestic energy	42,585	76.0	43,812	12.0
Imported energy	13,431	24.0	322,829	88.0

Source: Agency of Natural Resources and Energy, Statistics of Energy, 1975.

This period coincides with the rapid growth period of the Japanese economy, and consumption of petroleum showed an enormous increase, factories switching from coal to petroleum for their power. Power stations also switched over from water power to thermal power, and the main raw material of the chemical industry became naphtha, an extract from petroleum. The amount of energy consumption in the fiscal year 1973 was 3,825 x 10^{12} Kcal. The details were 3.8% of domestic coal and 4.6% of domestic water power against 89.9% of overseas energy, comprising 77.4% of imported petroleum and 11.7% of imported coal, a dramatic decline in the position of domestic energy (Table 22). This decline in energy self-sufficiency was extraordinary, even in comparison with European countries, and Japan found itself dependent on OPEC countries, particularly the Middle East, for energy. The core of the energy industry changed from the coal industry, controlled by such Zaibatsu as Mitsui, Mitsubishi and Sumitomo, to the oil refinery industry, influenced by major foreign groups such as Exxon, Caltex, Mobil, Shell and so on, and the electric power industry, controlled by nine companies based on a special law.

COAL

In 1961 Japanese coal production reached 54,484 thousand tons, its peak after World War II, but thereafter decreased rapidly in the 'energy revolution' and totalled only 18,999 tons in 1973. During the 20 years from the end of 1955 to the end of 1975, the number of coal mines decreased from 742 to 36 and the number of workers from 286 thousand to 229 thousand, both drastic decreases. Coal mines were closed in various places and many coal mine towns disappeared or decayed. When coal production was prosperous in the later 1950s it could be summarised as follows: the largest producing area was Chikuho coalfield (Kyushu region), with 28.7% of the national production (1957). The Chikuho coalfield was worked by many great Zaibatsu, such as Mitsui, Mitsubishi and Sumitomo, and also large local enterprises and medium and small firms, forming a typical pyramidal structure. This type of structure was characteristic of coalfields which had long been developed, such as Joban coalfield (Fukushima

Prefecture). There were also coalfields where production was wholly in the hands of medium and small firms. On the other hand, great Zaibatsu groups occupied an overwhelming position in the coalfields of Kyushu, such as Miike, Takashima and others, where they had monopolised the mining sections since early times. There were also some medium and small firms on the Ishikari coalfield (23.8%), the Kushiro coalfield and elsewhere in Hokkaido, which were developed by Zaibatsu capital during the 1910s and the 1920s. In general, the centres of coal production were located at both ends of Japan, in the south and the north, in Kyushu (Chikuho, Miike, Takashima and so on – 53.5%) and in Hokkaido (Ishikari, Kushiro, Rumoi – 30.8%), and the centres of consumption were in central Japan, including Keihin, Chukyo and Hanshin industrial regions. Long-distance transport of coal was therefore required from Kyushu to Hanshin and Chukyo and from Hokkaido to Keihin.

Coalfields with low productivity managed by medium and small firms were closed first when the 'energy revolution' brought depression to the coal industry. In many of these coalfields not only was productivity low and cost high, but the product was also poor in calorific value and in type, factors which hastened their run-down. The coalfields managed by large organizations began to reduce production from the end of the 1960s and soon almost all coalfields were approaching abandonment. By 1975 Ishikari's production had fallen to 48.9%, Kushiro's to 10.1%, Miike's to 28.2% and Takashima's to 8.8%, (Fig 4.4) yet these four coalfields, managed by large organizations, produced 96% of total output. Almost all other coalfields had gone out of production.

The demand for coking coal during this period increased from 43,465 thousand tons in 1955 to 81,705 thousand tons in 1975, and coal was heavily imported to make good the deficit of domestic coal. In these twenty years coal imports increased from 2,825 thousand tons to 62,398 thousand tons, a more than 20 times increase. The main sources of supply were Australia, the United States and Canada.

PETROLEUM

Crude oil production in Japan is extremely small, only 705

thousand kl in 1975, equivalent to 0.2% of total demand. Therefore, the increase in petroleum consumption meant a rapid increase in imports of crude oil. Imports of 9270 thousand kl in 1955 reached 28,670 thousand kl in 1973 and 262,806 thousand kl in 1975. By value imports of crude oil in 1975 reached 19,635 mil. dollars, and accounted for approximately 1/3 of total imports, 57,863 mil. dollars, and 15.4% of world trade in crude oil in that year.

Japan's major suppliers of crude oil are the Middle East, particularly Saudi Arabia and Iran, and south-eastern Asia, centring on Indonesia. Although the share of the Middle East has declined somewhat since the 'energy panic', it is still the highest (Table 23).

Most of this crude oil is supplied by the five major companies – Socal, Texaco, Exxon, Mobil and Shell. These major companies have joint oil refining companies with Japanese groups and sell their final products in Japanese markets. There are 15 of these refinery-sales companies in which foreign capital is represented: they belong to the four groups, Nippon Oil, Toa Nenryo Kogyo, Showa Oil and Mitsubishi Oil. The sixteen companies not coupled with foreign capital include Idemitsu Kosan, Kyodo Oil and Maruzen Sekiyu.

TABLE 23

Share of Japan's Crude Oil Imports by Area (1975)

	Thousand kl	Per cent
Saudi Arabia	67,081	25.5
Kuwait	22,594	8.6
Neutral Zone	13,449	5.1
United Arab Emirates	24,261	9.2
Iran	65,119	24.8
Others	13,099	5.0
Middle East total	205,603	78.2
Africa	7,585	2.9
Indonesia	30,032	11.4
Others	19,133	7.3
Asian total	49,165	18.7
Others	453	0.2
Grand Total	262,806	100.0

Source: Agency of Natural Resources and Energy, Statistics of Energy, 1975

These two groups are virtually equal in both refinery output and sales value.

Before and immediately after World War II works producing a range of products, such as gasoline, paraffin oil, light oil, fuel oil and so on, were located in oil field areas such as Akita and Niigata prefectures along the Sea of Japan and were of considerable importance. When, however, the proportion of overseas crude oil rose rapidly, the location of oil refineries was gradually concentrated in the Pacific Coastal Belt, for convenience of importing and of access to the major industrial regions, such as Keihin, Hanshi and Chukyo.

The Japanese oil refinery industry, which had 19 installations producing 285 thousand barrels per day in 1955, increased to 48 installations and 5860 thousand barrels per day at the end of 1975, a 2.5 times production capacity increase. The distribution of these factories can be summarised: the Tokyo Bay coastal areas and their surrounding areas, including the Keihin industrial region, 14 works, 2250 thousand barrels per day (38.5%); the Ise Bay coastal areas and their surrounding areas, including the Chukyo industrial region, 6 works, 840 thousand barrels per day (14.3%); the Osaka Bay coastal areas and their surrounding areas, including the Hanshin industrial region, 7 works, 720 thousand barrels per day (12.3%); and the Seto Inland Sea coastal areas, including the northern Kyushu industrial regions, 10 works, 1390 thousand barrels per day (23.6%). The concentration in the three bays and the Inland Sea in the Pacifc Coastal Belt reaches the high percentages of 77 in number of works and 89 in production capacity. Other locations include Sea of Japan coastal areas adjacent to domestic crude oil producing areas in Akita and Niigata Prefectures, 5 works, 140 thousand barrels per day (2.4%), Hokkaido and Tohoku District, 4 works, 310 thousand barrels per day (5.3%), and Okinawa in the south of Japan, 3 works, 210 thousand barrels per day (3.6%) (Fig. 4.4)

The selection of location of these works shows a characteristic tendency. The oil refining companies are roughly divided into seven groups, including foreign capital companies and national capital companies. Each of these groups had 1 or 2 oil refineries in a specific area and supplied the whole country from there before the 'energy revolution' became

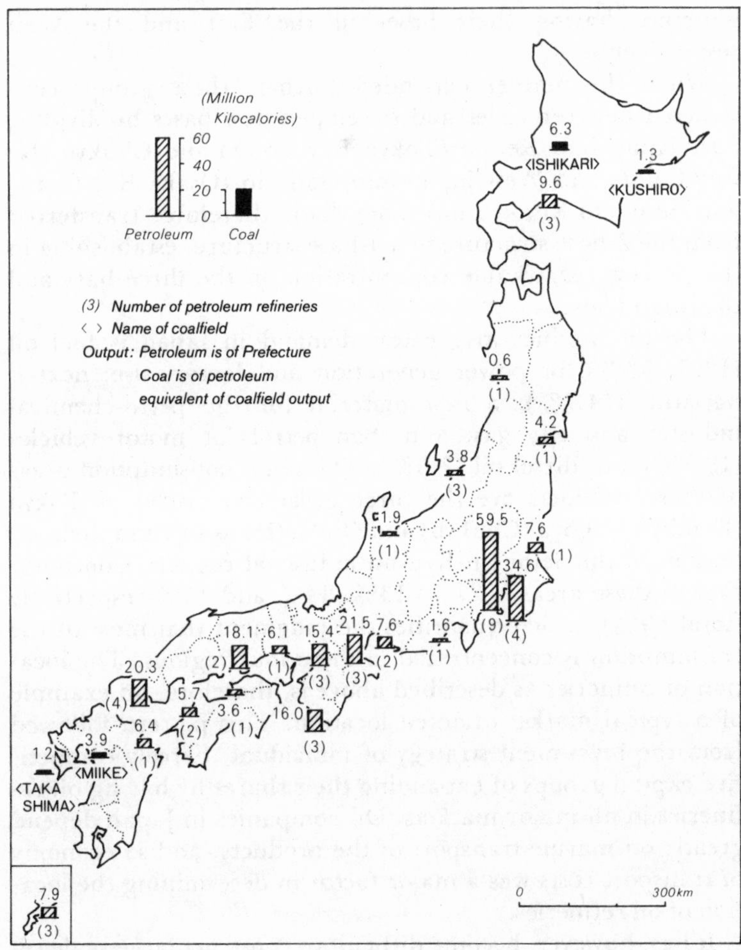

Fig. 4.4 Output of oil and coal. 1975 Fiscal Year

definite, but they began to construct new oil refineries in the Pacific Coastal Belt and at positions convenient for developing new markets when the oil market expanded and increase in the number of oil works became necessary. The groups with installations in Keihin, Chukyo and elsewhere in East Japan constructed new works in West Japan, and the groups which had their refineries in West Japan located their new ones in East Japan. As a result, the major groups established a 2-base structure having their bases in the East and the West respectively.

When the market expanded further, these groups constructed new refineries and developed new bases by dividing East Japan into Keihin (Tokyo Bay Coast) and Chukyo (Ise Bay Coast) and West Japan into Hanshin (Osaka Bay Coast) and Setouchi-Kitakyushu. They had, therefore, transferred from the 2-base structure to a 4-base structure, establishing in the process remarkable concentration on the three bays and the Inland Sea.

The oil product in greatest demand in Japan is fuel oil (1957, 53%) for power generation and factory use; next is naphtha (14.7%), a raw material for the petro-chemical industry and city gas, and then petrol for motor vehicles (13.7%) and diesel oil (7.5%). The main consumption areas of these products are the three great city circles of Tokyo (Keihin), Nagoya (Chukyo) and Osaka (Hanshin) and their extension in the Setouchi-Kyushu industrial regions. Consumption in these areas is 27%, 13%, 14% and 15% respectively (total 69%), which quantifies the judgment that most of the consumption is concentrated in these four regions. The location of refineries as described above is, therefore, an example of a typical market-oriented location. This pattern followed from the investment strategy of individual, fiercely competitive capital groups of expanding their shares by having oil refineries in all major markets. Oil companies in Japan depend greatly on marine transport of the products, and so economy of transport costs was a major factor in determining the location of oil refineries.

It has, however, become difficult to construct large-scale refineries in the Pacific Coastal Belt because of shortage of land and environmental problems. Plans have consequently been advanced to concentrate refineries in the south and the north ends of Japan, such as Hokkaido, Tohoku, Southern Kyushu and Okinawa, and some oil refineries are already located in these remote areas.

ELECTRIC POWER

The demand for electric power in the high economic growth period showed a growth as remarkable as that of oil, and power stations increased correspondingly. The 14,512 thousand kw of 1955 increased to 112,285 thousand kw in 1975, a 7.7 times increase during the twenty years, and in that time, hydro-electric power also gave way to thermal power. In 1955 water power produced 74.3% of the total power generated, and thermal power the rest, though 96% of the fuel in thermal power stations was still coal and fuel oil was almost negligible. Thermal power generation, however, increased rapidly along with the decrease in the cost of generation. The ratio between water power and thermal power was reversed in 1962, and thereafter thermal power dominance continued. Fuel oil progressively replaced coal and by 1975 their relative positions had been reversed. Furthermore, atomic power generation was started in 1966, and its weight increased gradually. In these circumstances the total power generation in 1975 consisted of thermal power 76.7%, water power 18.1% and atomic power 15.3%. The fuel for thermal power generation was provided by fuel oil, 92% and coal, 8%.

The electric power industry in Japan was managed by nine electric power companies. They divided the whole country into nine blocks, and each company performed generation, transmission, and distribution monopolistically in its own block. This organisation was set up by adminstrative order of the occupation forces in 1950, but with the return of Okinawa in 1972, the 10-company structure arrived. Each company had to increase its equipment to meet the demand in the area in its charge.

During the 1950s, when water power generation was dominant, huge dams were constructed in the mountains of Central Japan and the Tohuku region, and formed a great power generation area. In and after the 1960s, with generation being increasingly taken over by thermal stations, particularly oil-fired stations, large scale oil-fired thermal power stations were progressively constructed in large cities and large industrial regions. The location of these power stations was obviously aimed at easy access both to markets and also to oil refineries for convenience of supply of fuel oil.

In consequence, the concentration of thermal power stations in the three bays and one inland sea of Tokyo Bay coast, Ise Bay coast, Osaka Bay coast and the Seto Inland Sea coast repeats the distribution of oil refineries. The five electric power companies that operate in these areas have 68.1% of the total capacity of the ten electric power companies.

Many thermal power stations use fuel oil alone or a mixture of crude oil and fuel oil, but some stations in Hokkaido, Tohoku, Chugoki and Kyushu burn a mixture of coal and fuel oil, and some in Kanto and Kinki use liquified natural gas (LNG) for fuel. Recently construction of atomic power stations has been active, and at the end of the fiscal year 1976, 13 atomic reactors were operating at 8 power stations.

PERSPECTIVE

A review of the Japanese energy supply structure was stimulated by the 'energy panic' of 1973, and the government adopted the policy of promoting the use of coal and LNG as fuel for electricity generation. New power stations, therefore, are being constructed to use coal and LNG as fuel in large consumption areas. In addition, many plans for construction of atomic power stations have been promoted in various places. The execution of these plans, however, is largely delayed because of the residents' opposition to the expected environmental pollution. In particular, since construction of oil refineries and fuel oil thermal power stations has become extremely difficult in large cities, the government in its regional development policy is trying to encourage energy supply bases by developing remote areas such as Hokkaido, Tohoku and Kyushu. When this plan is actually implemented, new energy bases will be widely distributed along the coasts from the north to the south instead of the concentration on the three bays and one inland sea that now characterises the oil refineries and thermal power stations.

3

Iron and Steel

S. YAMAMOTO AND M. MURAKAMI

POSITION AND CHARACTER

In general, the iron and steel industry belongs to the most fundamental industrial sector, furnishing basic materials widely to various industries. The rapid growth of the Japanese economy after World War II was supported by the development of manufacturing industry, and the iron and steel industry played a central role in that development. Secondly, the international position of the Japanese iron and steel industry is also extremely strong. Japanese iron and steel production takes third position in the world, crude steel production being 107 million tons (1976), which follows USSR (approximately 145 million tons, 21.3% of world production) and the United States (approximately 116 million tons, 17.1%). Iron and steel production exceeded that of Britain in 1961 and that of West Germany in 1964 to reach this third position. The crude steel production index (1955 base 100) was 1142 in 1977, an extremely high development rate in comparison with 109 for the United States, 199 for West Germany and 111 for Britain. Further the industry is expanding its competitive power in international markets in parallel with the development of production: 34.5% of the crude steel production was exported in 1974. Japan has occupied the top position in the world for exports of iron and steel since 1969, and in 1974 contributed 26.2% of world exports of these commodities.

The third characteristic is that it is a typical oligopolistic industry: five major monopolistic groups headed by Nippon Steel Corporation control the whole industry, including the wide-ranging related industries. It has always been coupled with the State, as indicated by the saying 'iron is the State', and has developed under strong protection by the State. Its core was the Yahata Iron Works (present Nippon Steel Corporation).

TABLE 24

Change of Crude Steel Production in the World (1,000 ton)

	1955	1960	1965	1970	1975	1976	1976/ 1955
Japan	9,408	22,138	41,161	93,322	102,313	107,399	11.42
USSR	45,271	65,292	71,200	115,873	141,325	144,805	3.20
USA	106,173	91,920	119,016	119,308	105,818	116,122	1.09
W. Germany	21,336	34,100	36,816	45,041	40,415	42,415	1.99
China	2,853	16,500	12,000	17,400	26,500	26,000	9.11
Italy	5,395	8,229	12,660	17,277	21,837	23,446	4.35
France	12,592	17,300	19,608	23,774	21,530	23,221	1.84
Britain	20,108	24,695	27,432	28,316	19,780	22,396	1.11
World Total	270,400	346,700	455,000	595,200	646,900	680,600	2.52

Fourthly, the industry since the War has depended upon overseas countries, especially the United States, for important productive elements such as resources, techniques and capital.

The above-mentioned four points form an indispensable background for the study of the development and selection of location of Japan's iron and steel industry after the War.

DEVELOPMENT PROCESS

DEVELOPMENT BEFORE WORLD WAR II

The Meiji Government adopted policies for industrialisation with the slogans of 'promotion of industry' and 'national prosperity and defence', and established state enterprises, one such being the Kamaishi Mine (Iwate Prefecture), which produces good quality iron ore. At the Kamaishi Iron Works, iron was successfully manufactured by coke in 1894, with coal from the Yubari coalfield of Hokkaido. This laid the foundation for the modern Japanese iron manufacturing industry. The demand for iron and steel was increased by the military procurement demands, but the domestic production was not sufficient to fill the demand and iron and steel were imported, mainly from Britain. The self-sufficiency ratio in 1900 was 49.5% in pig iron but only 0.4% in steel.

Then the government determined to construct a state iron works, and the Yahata Iron Works started operation in 1901, using the integrated Steel Production System which had just been devised in Europe. In the period from the construction of the Yahata Iron Works to World War I the Japanese iron and steel industry was firmly founded, private enterprises which formed its core being successively established. The characteristics of this establishment period are at the same time the indices to the nature of the general development of capitalism in Japan. The first point is that the largest iron works was established by the state, not by private capital as in other advanced countries. The Yahata Iron Works was a product of the national policy of promotion of industrialisation and self-supply of materials for arms. The second is that private enterprises started their operation from steel making or rolling, which could be managed with comparatively little capital – they installed no blast furnaces but bought their pig iron from the Yahata Iron Works. The third is that the construction of iron works in overseas colonies such as Manchuria and Korea was started in the same period as in Japan proper.

The iron and steel industry, which was firmly established by World War I, carried on production under the thorough protection policies represented by the Act for Iron Production Promotion (1919), and in 1934 the Nippon Steel Corporation was created by the union of five private enterprises with the Yahata Iron Works. This great iron and steel trust produced 96% of the nation's pig iron, 53% of its crude steel and 44% of its steel materials.

DEVELOPMENT AFTER THE WAR

Before and after World War II the iron and steel industry depended upon raw materials from China and South East Asia, and developed on military demand, but it lost the basis for its development with Japan's defeat in the War. Although destruction by air-raids in the iron and steel industry was small in comparison with other industries, there were only three blast furnaces operating in the whole country at the end of 1946.

Thereafter, the industry gradually recovered till about 1950 with state financial assistance based on a priority production

TABLE 25

Integrated Steel Plants

	Name of Plant (Prefecture)	Quantity of Crude Steel Production (10,000 ton) 1975	Number of Workers 1975	Start of Production by Integrated System	Type of Location	Remarks
Nippon Steel	Muroran (Hokkaido)	307	6685	1941	A	1909 -- Blast furnace installed
	Kamaishi (Iwate)	109	4056	1903	A	
	Kimitsu (Chiba)	676	7936	1968	C	
	Nagoya (Aichi)	492	8735	1964	C	
	Sakai (Osaka)	311	3599	1965	C	
	Hirohata (Hyogo)	336	9383	1941	B	1939 -- Blast furnace installed
	Yahata (Fukuoka)	689	23597	1901	A	
	Oita (Oita)	294	3576	1972	C	
Nippon Kokan	Keihin (Kanagawa)	212	12802	1927	B	Consisting of 3 iron mills, each mill adopting the integration system in 1927, 1936, and 1962 respectively.
	Fukuyama (Hiroshima)	1233	12240	1966	C	

Sumitomo Metal	Kashima (Ibaraki)	497	6885	1971	C	
	Wakayama (Wakayama)	609	10445	1961	C	1942 -- Located as a steel plant
	Kokura (Fukuoka)	168	4225	1939	A	1916 " " "
Kawasaki Steel	Chiba (Chiba)	571	13906	1954	C	
	Mizushima (Okayama)	725	13062	1967	C	
Kobe Steel	Amagasaki (Hyogo)	39	1997	1941	B	1933 -- Located as a steel plant
	Kakogawa (Hyogo)	466	6685	1970	C	
	Kobe (Hyogo)	232	10094	1961	C	1905 -- Located as a steel plant
Nisshin Steel	Kure (Hiroshima)	255	10039	1962	C	1951 -- Located as a steel plant
Nakayama Steel	Osaka (Osaka)	90	3145	1939	B	1933 -- Located as a steel plant
Osaka Steel	Osaka (Osaka)	53	1496	1960	C	1934 -- Located as a steel plant

Sources: Statistical Handbook of Steel, Yearbook of Steel.
Type of Location: A . . . . . Material orientation
B . . . . . Market orientation
C . . . . . Post-war location

system and then was greatly stimulated by the special procurement caused by the Korean War (1950–1). The foundations for today's development were laid by successive renewal of plant and by innovation. Firstly, an integrated production system was promoted by the systematic carrying out of the scrap-and-build policy in compliance with the first stage rationalisation plan (1951–5), the second stage rationalisation plan (1956–60) and the third rationalisation plan (1960–).

The pre-war Nippon Steel Corporation was divided into two companies, Yahata and Fuji, by the occupation policy, and the Kawasaki Iron Works, Sumitomo Metal Industries and Kobe Steel which had been open-hearth furnace steel makers, built new integrated works.

Secondly, from 1955 heavy new investment expanded the production capacity to match the renewal of equipment and the innovation elsewhere in the world and the expected tremendous increase of the demand for steel. The strip-mill was introduced in the rolling process. The most advanced blast furnaces were built for pig iron production and the LD converter was introduced in steel making. Concurrently rationalised control of reception of order, production plan, process control and stock control by computers was completed. The effect of these measures was to provide the iron and steel industries of Japan with high productive and strong international competitive power.

Thirdly, the iron and steel enterprises undertook construction of new and powerful iron works under the third stage rationalisation plan from the beginning of the 1960s and formed iron and steel supply bases in the Pacific Coastal Belt, where locational conditions are favourable, but this will be dealt with more fully later.

LOCATION AND DISTRIBUTION

DISTRIBUTION OF IRON AND STEEL PLANTS

As of 1977, there are 21 integrated steel plants, and Table 25 shows their production scales and number of workers. Five major enterprises produce 77.3% (1976) of total crude steel production. Their leading six plants producing more than 5 million tons each of crude steel per year are the Fukuyama Plant of Nippon Kokan, the Mizushima Plant of Kawasaki Steel, the Yahata and the Kimitsu Plants of Nippon Steel, the Wakayama Plant of Sumitomo Metal and the Chiba Plant of Kawasaki Steel.

As is clear from Table 25, crude steel production is concentrated in Southern Kanto, Hanshin and the Seto Inland Sea Coast. We now consider circumstances related to the selection of location in each period.

CHARACTERISTICS OF PRE-WORLD WAR II TYPE LOCATIONS

The oldest iron works in Japan were located in Kamaishi and Yahata, the most important locational conditions being the presence of raw materials. The Yahata Iron Works was constructed to use the local coal of the Chikuho coalfield and the iron ore of Kamaishi,[1] and the Kamaishi Iron Works used the local iron ore and the coal of Hokkaido, Muroran Iron Works was built to use the ore and coal of Hokkaido.

These iron works, which formed the basis for Japan's iron manufacturing industry, are examples of materials orientation, attracted by the presence of domestic resources. This type of location, which was firmly established from the middle of the Meiji Era to the Taisho Era, was the same as that of advanced industrial countries such as Britain, Germany and the United States.

The surge of development of the iron and steel industry between the two world wars saw new works built in large industrial regions such as Keihin and Hanshin. From 1920 the location of the industry was changing to market orientation: production of raw materials, particularly of ore, was too small to fill the demand, and Japan had to depend upon China, Malaysia, the Philippines, India and others. Between 1935 and 1940, Nippon Kokan constructed integrated steel plants in Keihin and Nippon Steel Corporation in Hanshin. In this period five or six open-hearth furnace plants were located in the Hanshin region, and they developed into one integrated

[1]The Yahata Iron Works used Chinese ore and coking coal after the Sino-Japanese War (1894-5).

steel plant after World War II. This conversion to market orientation conformed to the circumstances of Japan with its poor raw material resources and extreme dependence upon overseas resources, but did not occur in Europe or the United States before the war.

POST-WAR TYPE OF LOCATION

The First Period (1950-60). The iron and steel industry after the War was developed by the construction of most advanced iron works based on rationalisation plans.

During the first stage rationalisation plan, the main activity was to adopt new techniques, scrap the old plant and equipment and build new ones. Two new trends were seen in the later 1950s. The first was initiated by the decision of the open-hearth steel makers to construct blast furnaces and establish an integrated steel production system. These companies, mainly Sumitomo Metal Industries, Kobe Steel, Osaka Steel, Nisshin Steel and Nakayama Steel, developed their plants into large-scale integrated steel plants in the late 1950s and the early 1960s. What they did, however, was to expand the plants already located in the Keihin and Hanshin industrial regions, not to initiate new location of plants.

The second trend was that new plants were constructed in the coastal areas of the Keihin and Hanshin regions. The Kawasaki Steel Corporation constructed its pig and steel plant in Keihin and Sumitomo Metal Industries and Kobe Steel built their pig and steel plants in Hanshin region, and had completed construction by the early 1960s. These new plants were located within the two large industrial regions or in their outer rings, inheriting the pre-war locational type of market orientation.

The Second Period (1960-). The new selection of location after the War reflected the third stage rationalisation plan. Large-scale plants with a production capacity of ten million tons per year were successively built in areas away from Keihin and Hanshin regions under the economic growth policy of the 1960s. Eight plants were constructed during the 1960s with the equipment investment exceeding three billion yen, and in each the blast furnace capacity was enlarged, seeking large scale economy. In pre-war Japan the largest blast furnace capacity was $1000m^3$, but a blast furnace of $2000m^3$ capacity started operation in 1964. The capacity exceeded 4000^3 in the beginning of the 1970s and is now 5000^3. As of 1976, there were 15 blast furnaces in the world with a capacity of more than $4000m^3$ and ten of them are in Japan.

Location characteristics of these new works may be noted.

Firstly, these integrated steel plants were all constructed on reclaimed land in coastal regions in the Pacific Belt Region, succeeding the pre-war market orientation type.

Secondly, this locational pattern, however, cannot simply be characterised as market orientation type. The raw material self-supporting ratio of the Japanese iron and steel industry in 1976 was: iron ore, 1.3%, and coking coal, 11.4%. The degree of dependence on overseas materials, therefore, is very high. These locations were obviously selected for their proximity to ports to cheapen the importing of raw materials. Location in a coastal area having superior port functions economises terminal costs and avoids the breakdown of transport. An import port is, so to speak, a source of supply of raw materials, and it is also a large market, including both domestic and export demand. The major industrial areas and their peripheral areas in the Pacific Coastal Belt have excellent locational conditions and are also positioned to enjoy great agglomeration advantages. These complex advantages attracted the iron and steel industry.

Thirdly, the location of the iron and steel industry was based on the regional policy. The development of the heavy and chemical industries after the War formed an industrial complex in which iron and steel, chemical, electric power, oil and other industries are technically linked. Such an expansion in the scale of production in the iron and steel industry required a tremendous area of land, water, port facilities and so on, and the State and local autonomous bodies prepared them according to the industrial inducement policy.

Fourthly, the location of the iron and steel industry after the War was based on a clear principle. For instance, the Kawasaki Steel Corporation, which was merely an open hearth steel maker in the Kinki Region before the War, first selected Chiba in Keihin Region after the war for its integrated steel production system, and then added Mizushima (Okayama Prefecture). Kawasaki Steel's building of the large plants in Chiba and Mizushima demonstrates her strategy of two production bases, one for the east market and one for the west market. Nippon Kokan, which has been producing iron and steel in Keihin region since before the war, enlarged its plant in Keihin after the War and constructed a large blast furnace in Fukuyama (Hiroshima Prefecture) in 1966 as its base in West Japan, thereby completing the east-west 2-base strategy. It also scrapped three obsolete plants in Keihin region and built a large new up-to-the-minute plant on an artificial island in Tokyo Bay.

The Nippon Steel Corporation became the largest steel corporation in the world by amalgamating Yahate Steel and Fuji Steel in 1970. The Yahata group had built new plant further east, to supplement the main plant at Yahata in Northern Kyushu, at Sakai (Osaka Prefecture, 1965) and at Kimitsu (Chiba Prefecture, 1968). In contrast the Fuji group, which had had works at Kamaishi in Tohoku and Muroran in Hakkaido, built new plant at Tokai (Aichi prefecture, 1964) and at Oita (east Kyushu, 1972) and moved westward in enlarging the Hirohata plant (Hyogo Prefecture). Sumitomo Metal Industries and Kobe Steel show the same trends in locational movement as were seen in the economic growth period. These trends were based on the policy that aimed at the reduction of distribution cost by arranging the plant location corresponding to the regional demand. The severe market competition by area among the large organizations clearly has an important role in the choice of location.

These locational tendencies can be recognised more or less clearly in other basic material production sectors, too. The heavy and chemical industries, which led the rapid economic growth, strengthened the agglomeration in the Pacific Coastal Belt as a whole, while involving the decrease of the relative status of pre-existing large industrial regions, the rise of the peripheral areas, and the rise of East Japan, particularly in the Kanto region, and formed the framework of the regional distribution of all industries.

PERSPECTIVE

The iron and steel industries have contributed to the growth of the Japanese economy by the regular supply of good quality, cheap steel to the home and foreign markets, thus supporting the development of major industries. The environment of the iron and steel industries, however, has drastically changed with the chronic stagnation of the economy initiated by the oil panic. Firstly, the demand for iron and steel fell, producing a great gap between demand and supply. Secondly, production costs jumped because of the rise of prices of the main raw materials and fuels and of the decrease of the operation ratio, which made management conditions in the iron and steel industries more difficult. Thirdly, trading conditions in iron and steel have been hit by the intensification of competition in export markets, limitation of imports of iron and steel in Europe and America, and the appreciation of the yen.

Although the iron and steel industries of Japan have depended on overseas resources, the lack of domestic resources has not always been an obstacle to the growth of the iron and steel industry. Three relevant points may be noted.

Firstly, large-scale development of iron ore has progressed in Latin America, Australia, Africa and elsewhere, and the developing countries are exporters of iron ore, since they have little export merchandise other than primary products.

Secondly, the iron and steel industries in Western Europe and the United States were built on ample domestic resources, but the dependence on imported resources is rising in all of them with the superannuation and exhaustion of their resources and with the growing demand for raw materials. In this respect Japan's disadvantage is being cancelled. In 1973 the dependence of the United States on overseas iron ore was 37.7%; of West Germany on iron ore 90.9% and on coal 7.9%; of Britain on iron ore 77.1%; and of France on iron ore 24.6%, on coal 28.4%, and these figures are rising. Thirdly, the advantages of long-haul economy grew with the increase in size and speed of ore carriers.

As pointed out already, the iron and steel industries after

the War installed the most advanced plant in the Pacific Coastal Belt and made a vigorous drive for markets. The Western European countries and the United States also increased their imports of iron ore, but many of the iron works, located with reference to procurement of domestic materials, were in inland regions. The additional transport costs of moving the imported raw materials from the ports to the inland regions, were reflected in the production cost. Some new plants have been located at the sea coast in Europe and the United States since the War but the traditional location pattern has not yet been basically changed.

Paradoxically, although after the War the Japanese iron and steel industries realised rapid growth at coastal locations, such locations were almost inevitable given the poverty of the country in raw material resources.

PART FIVE

Development and Distribution of the Main Manufacturing Industries — 2

1

Motor Vehicles

A. TAKEUCHI

POSITION AND CHARACTER

The development of the motor vehicle industry since 1960 is among the most remarkable in Japanese industry. The number of motor vehicles produced in Japan in 1958 was 188,000, only about 3.7% of production in USA, and little more than that percentage in West Germany, Britain or France. From the early 1960s, however, it showed a phenomenally high growth rate. Finally in 1970, it exceeded the Western European countries and in 1975 produced 6.95 million vehicles, 21% of world production. This is approximately 77.5% of the figure of the USA, the largest producing country in the world, and more than twice as many as the number in France, the largest producing country in Europe.

In the 1950s the motor vehicle industry was not conspicuous among Japanese industries, but it progressively improved its position until it claimed 8.4% of total industrial production in

TABLE 26

Motor Vehicle Production Numbers (1,000)

	1958	1963	1970	1975
U.S.A.	5,121	9,109	8,244	8,976
Japan	188	1,284	5,303	6,948
France	1,127	1,737	2,750	3,288
W. Germany	1,495	2,668	3,838	3,192
U.S.S.R.	511	633	870	1,966
Britain	1,364	2,012	2,097	1,656
Italy	404	1,181	1,855	1,453
Canada	360	763	1,191	1,424
Total*	11,289	20,690	28,410	32,900

Source: UN. Statistical Yearbook
*Total includes other countries excepting China

1975. This ranks it next to iron and steel (10%) as a single merchandise. The industry, including completed vehicle assembly works, parts factories, and body factories, employs in total 650,000 workers. It is a representative export industry in parallel with iron and steel and shipbuilding; with 14.5% of total export value it ranked next to iron and steel in 1975. With the remarkable development of the motor vehicle industry, the scale of the motor vehicle makers also grew. In particular the two major makers, Toyota and Nissan (Datsun), have become not only top enterprises in Japan but also great enterprises in the world. Among the motor vehicle-makers in the world, Toyota and Nissan take third and fourth places in the number of vehicles produced, following General Motors and Ford.

DEVELOPMENT

The industry began in 1910, and during 1924–5 Ford and General Motors established their assembly factories. In and after 1930 the Japanese government strengthened its policy of promoting production of domestic vehicles. First of all Nissan, which had been producing parts for Ford and General Motors, constructed a factory in Yokohama and started assembling itself, and in Chukyo region Toyota started production of motor vehicles, utilising the capital and technology obtained from its weaving machine production, and constructed a large factory in what is now Toyota City. The government controlled production by foreign companies in order to protect domestic enterprises, and since then Nissan and Toyota have been the core of motor vehicle production in Japan. Isuzu, which ranks next to these two companies, was established by amalgamation of small scale truck-makers in Keihin region.

The machinery industry in general, having lost the military procurement demand after World War II, was converted to peace-time industries. In the motor vehicle industry, aircraft-makers such as Mitsubishi and Nakajima, in addition to the existing makers such as Toyota, Nissan, Isuzu, Hino, turned to the vehicle industry, utilising their aircraft production techniques. The makers of 2-wheel and 3-wheel motor vehicles and light motor vehicles such as Toyo Kogyo, Honda and Suzuki developed into regular vehicle makers in the 1960s. After 1965 the Japanese motor vehicle industry faced severe international competition, following the transition to liberalisation of trade. The companies attacked this problem by investing tremendous amounts in plant and equipment aiming at reduction of costs by mass production. This brought about intensification of competition for domestic markets. In this situation Nissan and Toyota, the two major makers, constructed large factories in the peripheral areas of the existing industrial regions and steadily expanded their scale and increased their market shares. Furthermore, Toyota brought Daihatsu and Hino under its control, and Nissan brought Fuji under its control. On the other hand, Isuzu cooperated with General Motors and Mitsubishi with Chrysler in order to compete with Toyota and Nissan. Honda and Toyo Kogyo have continued their activities as independent makers thanks to their own high technology.

DISTRIBUTION AND LINKAGE

DISTRIBUTION

The motor vehicle industry is an assembly industry which assembles various processed materials and parts. Approximately 1500 parts of various kinds are required, and, indeed, on a more detailed classification, even 15,000 items. The motor vehicle works are classified according to the process into (i) assembly works, (ii) body works and (iii) parts works.

The industry is headed by a small number of completed vehicle assembly works, numbering 11 in 1975. Among them Toyota with 34% of total output, and Nissan with 30% were outstanding. They were followed by Toyo Kogyo (Mazda 9.3%), Mitsubishi (7.5%), Honda (6.0%), Suzuki (2.7%), Fuji (Subaru 2.5%), Hino and Nissan Diesel (1% each).

There are two major producing centres, Keihin region and Chukyo region, the former with 32% of the total number of factories and the latter with 19%. In addition, there are small producing areas in Hanshin region, Gumma and Tochigi prefectures in Northern Kanto, Shizuoka prefecture in Tokai region, Hiroshima and Okayama prefectures in the Seto Inland Sea region.

In the Keihin region are the 10 completed vehicle assembly

factories of Nissan, Honda, Isuzu, Hino and Mitsubishi, which together provide 45% of the shipment value of the whole country. Body factories number only 23% of the national total but account for 56% of the shipment value. The reason why the nationwide ratio of body production is high in Keihin region is that Toyota and Nissan are both represented there, and Toyota especially has large scale body factories for commercial and private vehicles. Parts factories are 36% of the nationwide number and shipment value is 42%. The characteristic of parts production in Keihin region is not only the large production amount but also the great variety of parts.

Chukyo region has assembly works of Toyota, Mitsubishi and Honda, which together contribute 30% of the national shipment value. They provide 20% in body production and 25% in parts production, but the variety of products is smaller

TABLE 27

Distribution of Motor Vehicle Factories 1974

		Completed Vehicle	Body	Parts
Northern Kanto	Ibaraki	0	1	19
	Tochigi	1	7	27
	Gumma	1	4	22
	(Sub-total)	2	12	68
Keihin	Saitama	2	4	38
	Chiba	0	0	10
	Tokyo	4	10	54
	Kanagawa	4	25	85
	(Sub-total)	10	39	187
Tokai	Shizuoka	2	5	37
Chukyo	Gifu	0	5	13
	Aichi	6	14	84
	Mie	1	2	13
	(Sub-total)	7	21	110
Hanshin	Osaka	1	4	30
	Hyogo	1	5	12
	(Sub-total)	2	9	42
Setouchi	Okayama	1	1	11
	Hiroshima	2	5	19
	Others	0	19	50
	TOTAL	28	121	524

Source: MITI, General List of Factories in Japan

than in Keihin region. Elsewhere, the position of Hanshin region in the national production is low, the only maker with an assembly works being Daihatsu. In Northern Kanto, motor vehicle factory distribution centres on Ota in Gumma Prefecture. These are the factories of Fuji (Subaru), established by Nakajima aircraft manufacturing company, which had been one of the two major aircraft makers in Japan until the end of World War II, when it entered the motor vehicle industry, producing 2-wheel motor vehicles and light motor vehicles. Nissan also has factories near Utsunomiya in Tochigi Prefecture. In addition, there is a bus body factory converted from aircraft production in Northern Kanto. The Shizuoka Prefecture percentage of the national production of completed vehicles is only 2%, which is produced by Suzuki, but parts factories supplying assembly works in Keihin and Chukyo are concentrated, and account for 10% of the national production. In the Seto Inland Sea region Mitsubishi, which produces small trucks, is located in Okayama Prefecture, and Toyo Kogyo (Mazda) has an assembly plant in Hiroshima; Hiroshima Prefecture produces approximately 10% of the national production of completed vehicles, and ranks next after Keihin and Chukyo. The number of parts factories, however is small and the proportion of the national shipment value is only 2%. Okayama Prefecture is similar. Elsewhere, some parts factories have moved to Southern Tohoku and Nagano Prefecture from Keihin region, but their production value is small.

INTER-REGIONAL LINKAGE

Generally the assembly works themselves produce some important parts, such as engines, transmissions, or others, and purchase the other parts from parts makers. The purchasing cost of parts is about 65% of total production cost and the cost of outside order processing 5%. Also, since assembly works are few in number, parts makers which at first glance look like independent enterprises have actually a sub-contracting character and are controlled by a few vehicle makers. A co-operators' society, which main sub-contractors join, is organised under each assembly plant but parts makers do not deliver their products to only one enterprise and often they belong to the co-operators' societies of two or three companies.

As already indicated, the distribution of completed vehicle production and the distribution of parts production differ considerably. Let us consider the regional relationship between the main assembly works and the parts makers.

First of all, Nissan, Isuzu, and Hino, which have factories in Keihin region, have almost all their sub-contractors in Keihin region. Toyota has its factories essentially concentrated in Chukyo region, and 54% of its sub-contracting factories are in the local Chukyo region, but 29% of its intake of parts comes from Keihin region.

Daihatsu in Hanshin region, has over half of its total sub-contractors in the local area, 17% in Keihin region and 10% in Chukyo region. Similarly Fuji (Subaru) in Northern Kanto has 60% in its local area and the rest in Keihin region. Suzuki in Shizuoka Prefecture has approximately half its sub-contractors in its local area; the rest are in Keihin and Chukyo regions. Toyo Kogyo (Mazda) in Hiroshima, which is remote from main industrial areas, orders 50% of its parts from outside, which is low compared with Nissan and Toyota. Since 90% of Toyo Kogyo's sub-contractor factories are in its local area, it looks as though the Toyo Kogyo is adopting a regionally self-sufficient production system, but the company does purchase parts from related factories in Keihin and Chukyo. The range of parts that can be supplied by local sub-contractors is limited, and production in this remote area must depend on Keihin and Chukyo.

TWO LARGE PRODUCING CENTRES – KEIHIN AND CHUKYO

(a) Keihin Region. The motor vehicle factories in Keihin, which is the largest producing centre, are distributed over a considerable area, as Fig. 5.1 indicates, but approximately 40% of them are concentrated in the district from the southern part of Tokyo to Kawasaki and Yokohama. Approximately 80% of motor vehicle factories were in the southern part of Tokyo before World War II and up to the 1950s. In and after the 1960s, Nissan, Honda, Isuzu and Hino constructed large factories in the peripheral areas of Keihin, and they became main factories. Now southern Tokyo has only two large completed vehicle truck factories. Some parts factories and body factories, similarly enlarged in scale, were also trans-

ferred from southern Tokyo to the peripheral areas of Keihin region. Southern Tokyo consequently lost its leading position in Keihin region, but the role played by the parts makers group in southern Tokyo has not changed at all. As Fig. 5.2 shows, the assembly works of Nissan, Isuzu, Hino and Mitsubishi in Keihin region have over half their total subcontractors in southern Tokyo. Now, 94% of the parts fac-

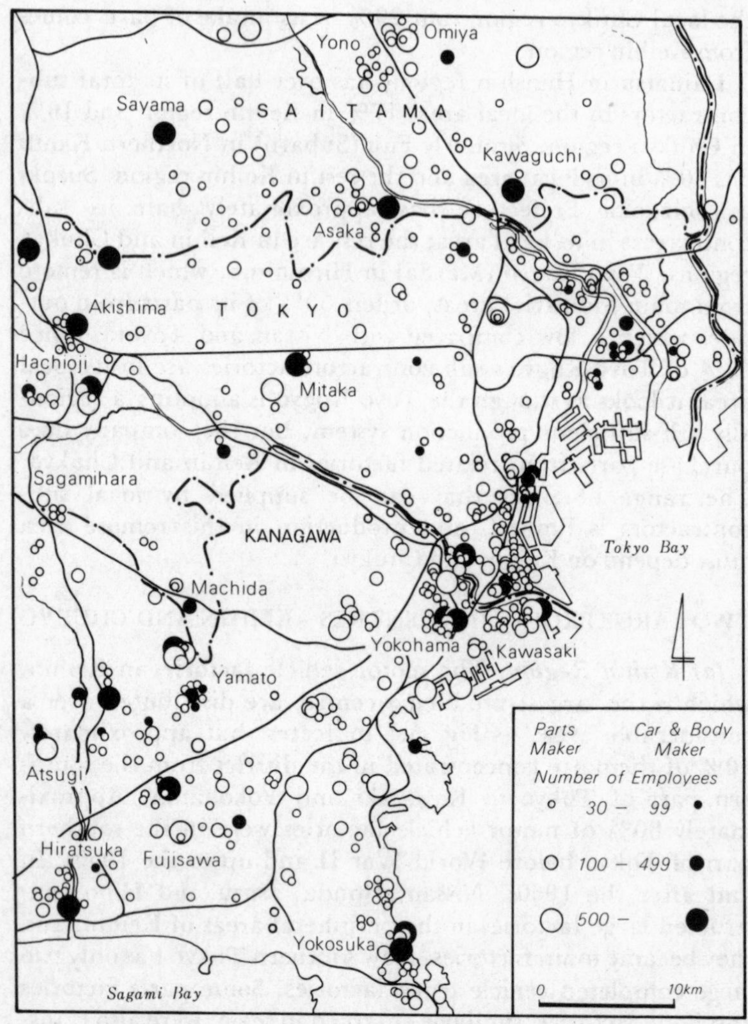

Fig. 5.1 Distribution of motor vehicle industry in Keihin region, 1969

tories further have sub-contractors under them, on average 40 per company, and purchases from these secondary sub-contractors accounts for 30% of the production cost. Approximately 70% of these secondary sub-contractors to the parts factories are concentrated in southern Tokyo. Groups of high technical competence have been formed in Southern Tokyo for mechanical operations such as pressing, mechanical processing, plating and so on. Accordingly, the large factories transferred to the peripheral areas of Keihin must still maintain constant linkage with the factory groups in southern Tokyo. So Keihin region has its large-scale assembly works in

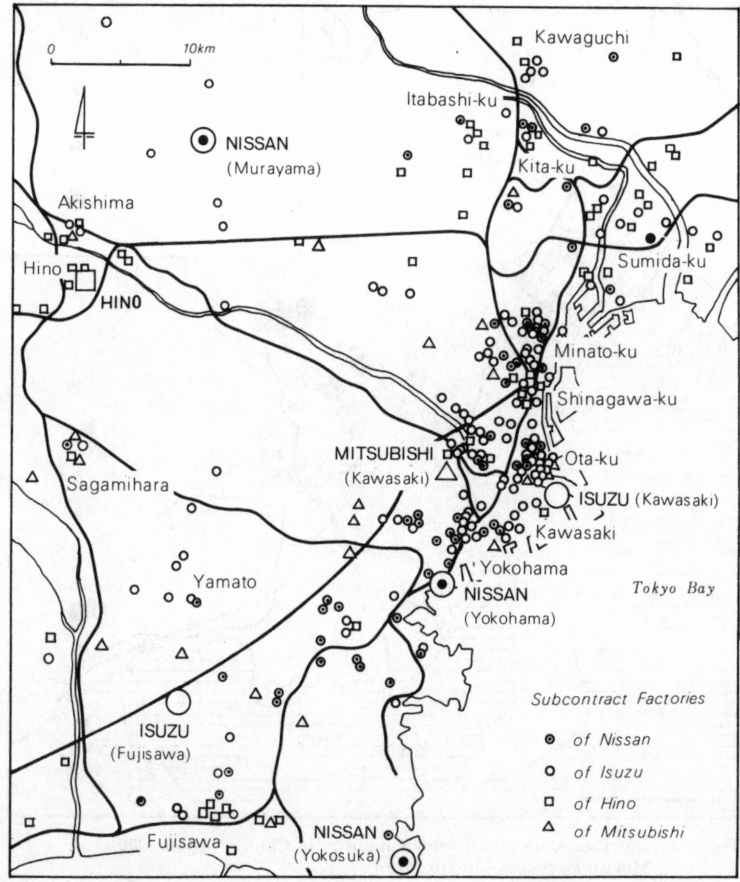

Fig. 5.2 Distribution of subcontracting in Keihin region, 1972
Kita-*ku* means Kita *Ward*

the outer ring, its parts factories and small scale sub-contract factories in the inner area, and they form a closely-linked regional production system.

(b) Chukyo Region. As Fig. 5.3 shows, there are two groups of factories in Chukyo region, which is the second motor vehicle producing centre. One centres on Nagoya, where machinery industries had been located since the Meiji Era, and Mitsubishi turned to motor vehicle production from aircraft production after World War II. The second group centres on Toyota.

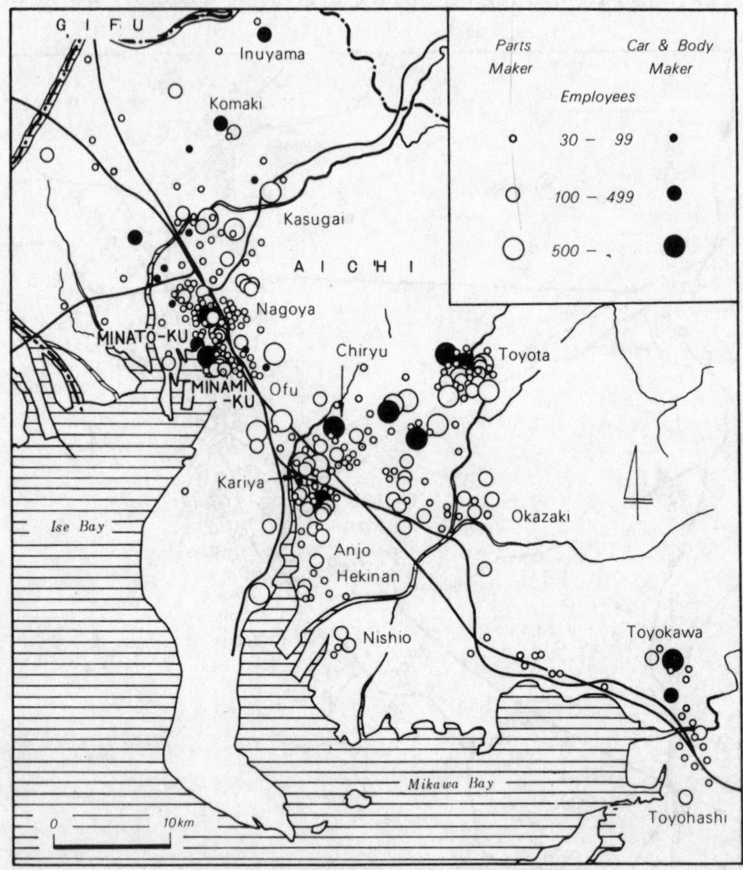

Fig. 5.3 Distribution of motor vehicle industry in Chukyo region 1970
Minato-*ku* means Minato *Ward*

What characterises motor vehicle production in Chukyo region is Toyota City, which is essentially a single industry town. Toyota City was a small old castle town, formerly called Koromo, but after Toyota arrived in 1938 it developed as Toyota's industrial town. In particular, from around 1955 Toyota successively constructed large works for passenger vehicles, and many parts factories were also located there. At present, out of approximately 2 billion yen worth of industrial production by Toyota City (1975), 95% is provided by Toyota and its sub-contractors, and these factories employ approximately 90% of the total industrial workers in the city. Toyota contributes 55% of the tax income of the city and has enormous influence in the municipal politics and economy and in all phases of the citizens' lives. Many parts factories of the Toyota Group are located in Kariya City, adjacent to Toyota City and account for almost the entire industrial production of Kariya City. It is not true, however, that the assembly works of Toyota find all their necessary parts in the local area. 35% of its sub-contractors are in Nagoya City and, further, most of the secondary sub-contractors are in southern suburbs of Nagoya.

MARKET STRUCTURE

The number of motor vehicles sold in Japan in 1975 was 4.320 millions, of which 600,000 were light motor vehicles. The demand for motor vehicles showed, temporarily, a drastic reduction following the oil panic, but thereafter grew agreeably despite the chronic depression and the regulations governing exhaust gas, which are the strictest in the world. Of the passenger vehicles, small cars and popular cars form 87% of the total vehicles sold. Toyota Carolla, with 650,000 vehicles produced per year and Sunny of Nissan (Datsun) are competing for top position among the mass production cars in the world. The number of imported motor vehicles, supported by government policy is increasing, and now amounts to 1.7% of the vehicles sold in Japan. Approximately 40% of the imported vehicles are Volkswagen of West Germany, and Ford and General Motors of USA follow.

The number of exported motor vehicles was only 38,000 in

1960, but increased to 2.680 million vehicles in 1975, which was 38.6% of total production. The number of motor vehicles exported is the highest in the world, far exceeding the figures for France, West Germany and USA. The ratio of export against production, however, is lower than in West European countries such as France, West Germany, Italy and Britain. The importers of these exported vehicles are, in order, North America (37.6%), Europe (19.7%), South-East Asia, West Asia and Oceania. Among countries USA comes first (34%), but Australia, Saudi Arabia, Britain and South Africa are also large importers. In the American market Japanese suppliers have outdistanced the formerly dominant Europeans and now account for more than half the total imported vehicles. In recent years developing countries with improving industrialisation have been importing cars in knock-down condition for local assembly. In 1975, the knock-down vehicles export was 20% of the total export, 67% for South-East Asia, 57% for Africa and 48% for Oceania. Toyota has 14 assembly factories in foreign countries. The proportion of knock-down cars, however, is low in North America and European countries.

2

Shipbuilding

S. YAMAMOTO

POSITION AND CHARACTER

Shipbuilding industry is the general term which includes construction and repair of vessels. Its structure is complex and varied. In comparison with shipbuilding in other advanced countries, the following four points are important.

Firstly, many of the Japanese shipbuilding companies are also 'collective heavy machinery industry' companies. This is an inheritance from historical conditions peculiar to the development of capitalism in Japan. The Japanese shipbuilding industry was started by the industrialisation policy of the Meiji government, though related industries were not yet adequately developed, and therefore necessary parts had to be produced in the shipbuilding yards themselves. In other words, the shipbuilding industry of Japan had to be a collective machinery industry from the start, and various machinery sectors and other related industries were later gradually organised from inside the shipbuilding industry. The fact that the industry still strongly retains the character of the collective machinery industry is a style peculiar to Japan.

Secondly, the Japanese shipbuilding industry is an oligopolistic sector with seven major enterprises dominating the industry. There are approximately 1,500 shipbuilding companies, 1,600 related industrial companies, 4,000 sub-contractors, 184,000 shipbuilding employees in the country. If the workers of sub-contractors and employees of related industries are included, the number of persons engaged in the shipbuilding industry reaches 361,000 (1975). Enterprises with the capacity to build vessels of over 10 thousand gross tons, however, number only 42. Nine medium and numerous small shipbuilding companies are affiliated to the seven major companies. The concentration of production in these major companies and their groups increased from around 1960, and reached 85.7% in 1970 and 95.9% in 1974. The largest are Mitsubishi Heavy Industry (26%) and Ishikawajima-Harima Heavy Industry (IHI, 20%).

Thirdly, as already mentioned, the shipbuilding industry is related to many other industries, the relationship with the iron and steel industry being particularly close. Since purchased steel accounts for approximately 25% of the production cost of a new vessel, the trend of the price of steel obviously has great influence on the industry. In this respect, the industry has the advantage of obtaining good-quality, cheap steel from the systematised steel makers. From the steel makers' side, 35% of the heavy steel sheet consumed in Japan was supplied to the shipbuilding industry, and the development of shipbuilding notably enlarged the market for the iron and steel industries. The efficiency of the iron and steel industries is clearly one factor in the strong international competitive power of the Japanese shipbuilding industry.

Fourthly, the Japanese shipbuilding industry specialises in certain kinds of vessel. Tankers, especially very large crude oil carriers (VLCC) and ultra large crude oil carriers (ULCC) (72.3%, 1975) rank high: more than half the tankers built in the world are constructed by Japanese shipbuilding yards. (In construction of liquefied petroleum gas carriers and container vessels, West Germany and Britain have high percentages.)

DEVELOPMENT AFTER THE WAR

Shipbuilding recorded remarkable development in the rapid economic growth period after the war. In 1956 it took top position in the world by exceeding that of Britain. Since then it has maintained its position, and the shipbuilding output in 1975 of 17,990 thousand gross tonnage was 50.1% of world production. The vessels further contributed greatly to the exports of Japan, becoming one of 'the big three' with iron and steel and motor vehicles. Three factors made this development possible.

Firstly, freight to be transported increased with the development of world trade, and the demand for vessels accordingly increased remarkably. The impact on shipbuilding of the increase in the demand for oil because of the world-wide energy revolution from the end of the 1950s, was particularly powerful. Large oilfields were developed in the Middle East and elsewhere, and the oil trade increased remarkably. For example, the amount of oil transported in the world multiplied 2.4 times between 1964 and 1974. So the marine transport business demanded ever larger tankers in order to lower transport costs, and in fact the size of vessels was progressively enlarged. The Japanese shipbuilding industry took positive and effective measures to meet this increased demand for tankers and so by the mid-1960s had established its position as the main world supplier.

In the early 1970s a tanker boom exceeding that of the 1960s occurred. In particular, in 1972 and 1973, immediately before the oil panic, orders for new vessels boomed, reaching a total of 54.14 million gross tonnage. Japanese shipbuilding enterprises continued investment in plant and equipment to cope with expansion in the demand for vessels and proceeded with construction of very large vessels.

The second factor was the revolution of shipbuilding technology, and in this the Japanese were pioneers in technical innovation. One of the important new techniques was the assembly-line operation system, called 'block building'. It was first attempted in 1949, was established by 1954, and spread to the shipbuilding yards in the whole country. This method differs from the traditional layer building method. The shell is divided into several blocks, which are loaded on the stock by large-size cranes after being assembled on the ground. Electrical welding became universal. Furthermore, in and after 1965 the Electronic Photo Marking Device (EPM) and the Number Control Cutting Machine were adopted. The introduction of these new techniques made shipbuilding with a short delivery term and low cost possible, by economising on the consumption of steel, lightening the body of the vessel and increasing loading capacity.

The third factor was the easy procurement of skilled labour forces at low wages. Needless to say, the shipbuilding industry depends upon intensive use of labour. Accordingly, its costs are characterised by a high relative proportion of labour and a low relative proportion of capital. Any change of wage level, therefore, directly influences the supply price of vessels, which in turn immediately acts upon international competitive power. Since rationalisation of agricultural management in the 1960s migration of labour from rural to urban areas has progressed nationwide, which enabled the shipbuilding industry to secure stable labour forces comparatively easily, as indeed did other industrial sectors. As the wage level increased, the securing of the necessary labour became more difficult, since shipbuilding work is often heavy, dirty and dangerous as compared with work in other industries. The shipbuilding industry has to face the difficulty of the upsurge of the 'the third group', which has cheap labour forces. That is why it is called a 'middle developed country' type industry.

DISTRIBUTION AND LOCATIONAL CHANGE

(a) Distribution. As previously mentioned, shipbuilding yards total approximately 1,500. Among them, those having ten or more employees are shown by scale in Table 28. Medium and small shipbuilding yards, which build and repair small cargo ships, fishing boats and special vessels for local markets are distributed nationwide. Column D indicates the distribution of yards catering mainly for local demands, such as short distance marine transport, fishing bases and the like.

We may note three points: (1) shipbuilding yards for building and repair of fishing boats reflect location of the fishery industry and are prominent in Hokkaido, Tohoku, Shizuoka, Mie and Nagasaki. (2) the distribution of the shipbuilding that catered from time immemorial for the Inland Sea traffic has been inherited in the various prefectures along the coasts of the Seto Inland Sea, and (3) large shipbuilding yards, A–C classes, show concentration in large city type industrial regions in Keihin and Hanshin and the Seto Inland Sea coasts. The distribution of the smallest yards, Column E, which are comparatively concentrated in Hokkaido, Hanshin, Sanyo and Kyushu, resembles that of the D class, but is more scattered since the E class yards are more strongly tied to purely local requirements. There is only an occasional one elsewhere.

(b) Pre-war Location. The general pattern combined two ele-

ments. The first was the separated individual shipbuilding towns. Nagasaki (north-west Kyushu), Innoshima and Kure (Hiroshima Prefecture), Aioi (Hyogo Prefecture), Maizuru (Kyoto Prefecture, facing the Sea of Japan), Tamano (Okayama Prefecture) and Hakodate (South Hokkaido). These towns, whose local economies were supported by the shipbuilding industry, were effectively 'single industry towns'. The other element, and the main one, was those which located in large industrial regions such as Hanshin and Keihin. In particular, the Hanshin region had many medium-sized yards in addition to the leading yards of Hitachi, Mitsubishi, and Kawasaki. Many of the yards were concentrated along the River Kizu above the inner end of Osaka Bay, producing a landscape reminiscent of that of the pre-war Clyde Valley in Scotland.

(c) Postwar Location. The pre-war locational pattern was

TABLE 28

Distribution of Shipbuilding Yards by Scale, 1974

Area	Number of workers A Over 1,000	B 999–500	C 499–200	D 199–50	E 49–10	Total
Japan	46	21	39	193	578	877
Hokkaido	3	1	2	6	60	72
Tohoku		2		23	38	63
Kanto (Keihin)	10	2	8	18	69	107
Hokuriku	1	1		2	22	26
Tokai	3	4	1	19	38	65
Kinki (Hanshin)	10	1		24	81	116
Sanin				6	13	19
Sanyo	12	5	11	42	107	177
Shikoku	2	3	10	25	70	110
Kyushu-Okinawa	5	2	7	28	80	122
Major Prefectures						
Chiba	1	1	3	6	19	30
Tokyo	2	1	1	1	24	29
Kanagawa	7		4	11	26	48
Osaka	6			3	7	11
Hyogo	3			14	49	66
Hiroshima	8	4	6	21	43	82
Yamaguchi	3		3	13	54	73
Nagasaki	5		3	10	25	43

Source: MITI, General List of Factories

largely changed with the remarkable development of shipbuilding after the War. Seven large capital groups located shipbuilding yards nationwide, each group aiming at a system of regional specialisation.

This process of location change may be divided into four periods, the first to the end of the 1950s, the second the first half of the 1960s, the third the latter half of the 1960s and the fourth period the 1970s.

In the first period no new location appeared, but the shipbuilding enterprises strove to restore the production capacity of existing yards and to improve their plant and equipment, and the old techniques were modified by innovations such as superseding riveting by welding (1950–2), and changing from the layer building method to the block building method (1950–60), among others, which permitted building of bigger ships.

In the second period, amalgamation of enterprises and selection of new locations were started. Ishikawajima Heavy Industry company and Harima Shipbuilding company were amalgamated to become Ishikawajima-Harima Industry (IHI) (1960), and three companies of the old Mitsubishi group were amalgamated to form Mitsubishi Heavy Industry (1963). Later IHI absorbed Nagoya Shipbuilding (1964) and Kure Shipbuilding (1968), thereby becoming the largest shipbuilding heavy machinery trust in Japan. As for new location, Mitsui located in Chiba, Hitachi in Sakai (Osaka Prefecture) and IHI in Yokohama.

The selection of location in this period showed a tendency for each capital group to keep a regional balance. For instance, Mitsui, which had a shipbuilding yard in Tamano (Okayama Prefecture), located a new yard in Chiba, and IHI, which was constructing a yard at Aioi (Hyogo Prefecture), decided to locate another new yard in Yokohama.

When the third period started in the later 1960s the selection of location of shipbuilding enterprises included not only absorption but also intensification of affiliation of medium and small companies. Mitsui became established in Osaka by absorbing Fujinagata Shipbuilding (1967) and Hitachi in Maizuru (Kyoto Prefecture) by absorbing Maizuru Shipbuilding (1970); but most of the existing medium and small companies were systematised under the control of the seven major enterprises. Among the major group, new yards were laid down by Kawasaki Heavy Industry at Sakaide on the Seto Inland Sea, by Nippon Kokan at Tsu on Ise Bay, and by Mitsubishi Heavy Industry and Hitachi Shipbuilding at Koyagi and Ariake respectively, in north-west Kyushu. Sumitomo and IHI constructed new large yards adjacent to the sites of their old works, which they abandoned. A characteristic of this period is that Sumitomo and IHI apart, the new large yards were often located in remote areas. This was because the physical location conditions for yards large enough to permit construction of the enormous vessels being demanded had to be satisfied even at the sacrifice of the agglomeration advantage, especially closeness to related industries.

In the fourth period, the 1970s, almost every enterprise in the major group announced construction plans for shipbuilding yards in Kyushu. Many of these plans are suspended under the continuing structural business depression that followed the oil panic. Since, however, Kyushu has the following advantages, it may well become a shipbuilding centre in the future.

1. Kyushu's mild, warm climate is convenient for the shipbuilding industry, which involves much outdoor work.

2. The necessary areas of land in the peripheral areas of large industrial regions and the Seto Inland Sea coasts because of the enlargement of stocks and docks are now difficult to find.

3. Kyushu can still supply local labour, but labour is now almost unobtainable in the existing industrial regions.

4. Since the markets for shipbuilding related industries have spread nationwide and the technical skill in related industries is disseminating into local areas, the location of the industry even in remote areas has become possible.

5. Shipbuilding has a considerable effect on employment and does comparatively little pollution damage, and so the local autonomous bodies are eager to attract the industry.

Within these location trends the strategy of the seven major groups is rounded off by a system of regional division of labour. IHI, for instance, has two shipbuilding yards each in Setouchi, Chukyo, Tokai and Keihin and the regional balance is maintained. The company regionally allocates the production to each shipbuilding yard according to the kind and size

TABLE 29

Regional Allocation of Shipbuilding Yards

	KYUSHU	SETOUCHI	HANSHIN	CHUKYO, TOKAI	KEIHIN	HOKKAIDO, TOHOKU, SEA OF JAPAN SIDE
Mitsubishi	Nagasaki Koyagi ('72) Namura ('62)	Hiroshima Shimonoseki	Kobe		Yokohama	
IHI		Kure ('68) Aioi ('60)		Nagoya ('64) Chita	Tokyo Yokohama '62	
Hitachi	Ariake	Innoshima	Sakai '62 Mukojima			Maizuru ('72)
Sumitomo			Sanoyasu ('68) Osaka Zosen ('72)		Uraga Oppama '72	
Kawasaki		Sakaide '65	Kobe			
Mitsui		Tamano	Fujinagata '67		Chiba '60	
Nippon Kokan	Sasebo ('66)			Shimizu '69 Tsu '69	Yokohama	Hakodate ('72)

Note 1) Maximum stock building capacity: Not less than 200 thousand tonnage — ; 100–200 thousand tonnage ; 50– 100 thousand tonnage ; less than 50 thousand tonnage

2) Years: built before the war; '62 newly built in 1962; ('62) under the control of the 7 major groups through absorption/affiliation.

of the vessels that have been ordered. For example, yards for super large vessels were constructed in Kure and Yokohama, those for 100 thousand tonnage class vessels and special vessels in Chita and Nagoya. The other capital groups have implemented similar schemes.

Table 29 indicates the regional allocation of main shipbuilding yards by each of the seven major groups. Each group has a main shipbuilding yard capable of building vessels of over 200 thousand tons and for other vessels the building bases are distributed nationwide depending on the size of the vessel.

MARKET STRUCTURE

The Japanese shipbuilding industry is an export industry. Eighty-two per cent of its output is for overseas markets, and of these exported ships, Liberia (42.7%) and Panama (7.6%) the chief 'flag of convenience' countries register almost exactly 50%. There has been a strong tendency in recent years for oil companies and mining companies to own their own ships, and these enterprises have therefore become part of the market.

Shipbuilding enterprises co-operated with shipping companies to secure domestic markets for vessels and with general trading firms for securing export markets, and these linkages are supported by banks. At the beginning of the 1960s the shipping business of Japan was concentrated into six groups under the guidance of the Ministry of International Trade and Industry, and concentration of the shipbuilding industry into seven groups was the industry's reaction to the shipping business reorganisation. As a result the domestic vessel market is almost stabilised, but competition for export orders is severe, and the cut prices of export vessels have sometimes caused friction between the shipbuilding industry in Japan and that of Europe.

With the change in ocean shipping conditions after the Suez Dispute, shipping companies aimed at reducing transport costs by employing larger vessels. At the same time, the market structure was changing, with transport of petroleum and iron ore increasing greatly. The Japanese shipbuilding industry consequently experienced an unprecedented demand for large tankers and the enterprises concerned were stimulated to build giant new shipbuilding yards, to expand their equipment, to undertake reorganisation by absorption or merger and systematise control, and to seek new locations for shipbuilding yards.

PERSPECTIVE

DIFFICULTIES AFTER THE OIL PANIC

The Japanese shipbuilding industry was comparatively stable for a long period, but it experienced serious structural depression after the oil panic of 1973. Ocean shipping slackened and in particular tankers became surplus to demand. In orders received, 33,800 thousand gross tonnage in 1973 was the peak, but this fell to 8,420 thousand gross tonnage in 1976, and no orders were received for large tankers. Moreover, for vessels already on order the purchasers often demanded cancellation of contracts or alteration of kind of vessel. The situation became so serious in 1975 that cancellations of contracts exceeded orders received.

This depression of the shipbuilding industry is serious for the regional economy. For example, Hashihama Shipbuilding (capital 22 hundred million yen, employees 800) on the Seto Inland Sea coast went bankrupt in 1977. Since the number of sub-contractors and related companies was 420 and the number of employees reached 8,500, the entire economy of the area suffered heavily.

Secondly, as the structural depression deepened, the competition between major enterprises for orders intensified, and small companies catering for the cargoboat market were hit particularly hard. The major enterprises began to tender for medium and small cargoboats, which had been a stabilised market for medium and small enterprises.

Thirdly, shipbuilding companies made strenuous efforts to increase their machinery production business, hoping to offset the shipbuilding depression by diversification.

Fourthly, they are applying rationalisation policies to curtail personnel, excessive equipment and so on. Despite all these efforts, Japanese shipbuilding has not yet got clear of the difficulties that occurred after the oil panic. On top of all that it is now facing a new problem: 'the third group', including especially the Republic of Korea, Brazil, Poland and Yugoslavia, have become powerful competitors against Japan and European countries. These countries had only 10% or so of the world's shipbuilding until the early 1970s, but they have caught up with the advanced shipbuilding countries, the figures showing 12% in 1975 and 20% in 1977. In orders received, as of June 1976, they showed 17,000 thousand gt (for 3.8 years) against 20,850 thousand gt (for 1.3 years) of Japan and 24,850 thousand gt (for 2.2 years) of the Association of West European Shipbuilders (AWES) countries. The Japanese shipbuilding industry, which not so long ago was outbidding the West Europeans with low prices and short term delivery, now faces the same difficult situation against these new competitors.

PART SIX

Industrial Location Policy and Environmental Issues

1

The Role of Industrial Location Policy

K. MURATA

The distribution of industry and the formation of industrial areas in Japan are not merely the results of free decision-making of private enterprises. Early in the Meiji Era the Government adopted positive protective development policies, which included attention to industrial location. In the depression of the 1930s industrial inducements were used to relieve the depression in the agricultural areas, and in World War II Government intervention aimed at decentralising industry in the interests of national defence. Some of those dispersed factories became nuclei for the development of new industrial areas. It was after 1960, however, that Government intervention became positive policy, and industrial location policy was linked with regional policy.

As Table 30 shows, the regional policy of Japan was based on the Comprehensive National Development Act, 1950, and in the 1950s development of power resources and elimination of bottlenecks in the main industrial regions became major objectives of the regional policy. In the 1960s it was the dispersal of manufacturing industry that became the major target.

As shown in Part 1, Chapter 1, the growth of industrial production after World War II was rapid, but it was realised through the revival of existing main industrial regions and expansion of their peripheral areas. Location policy was implemented by the Ministry of International Trade and Industry (MITI). But the *national* location plan did not then exist, and various policies were implemented by measures which were hardly more than tentative.

INDUSTRIAL LOCATION POLICY

NATIONAL INCOME DOUBLING PLAN

The National Income Doubling Plan 1960, was a long term economic development plan, which reflected developments after World War II in Japan. It aimed at continuing economic growth of 7.8% annually for ten years from 1960 to double the GNP *per capita* in 1970. The most important sector for this plan was manufacturing industry, which was expected to contribute growth of 9% yearly, with the 1970 output 3.3 times the output in 1960. In order to develop industrial production rapidly it was necessary to equip the production base at a highly effective location and to attract enterprises to such a location.

The region selected as fulfulling this requirement was the Pacific Coastal Belt. The reason for selecting this belt was explained as follows: Although industrial location is basically to be decided by enterprises on economic rationality, *laissez-faire* risks producing excessive expansion of urban areas and enlarging regional imbalance, with resulting impairment of national efficiency. On the other hand, if the balance between areas is over-emphasised and industries are dispersed into remote areas, economic development will be obstructed. It was this kind of thinking that led to the selection of the Pacific Coastal Belt as 'a place of effective dispersal', the main points for the selection being as follows:

1. The Pacific Coastal Belt is close to large markets and is well equipped with infrastructure. The presence of allied industries and sub-contract factories, too, adds to the locational advantages over other regions.

2. In four major industrial areas in the Pacific Coastal Belt, new location will be controlled and measures taken for promotion of efficiency and dispersal of industries to peripheral areas.

3. For the development of under-developed areas such as Hokkaido, Tohuku, the Sea of Japan, Coastal Belt, Southern Kyushu and others, industrialisation will be promoted after the completion of the National Income Doubling Plan: industrialisation of those remote areas before then would hamper

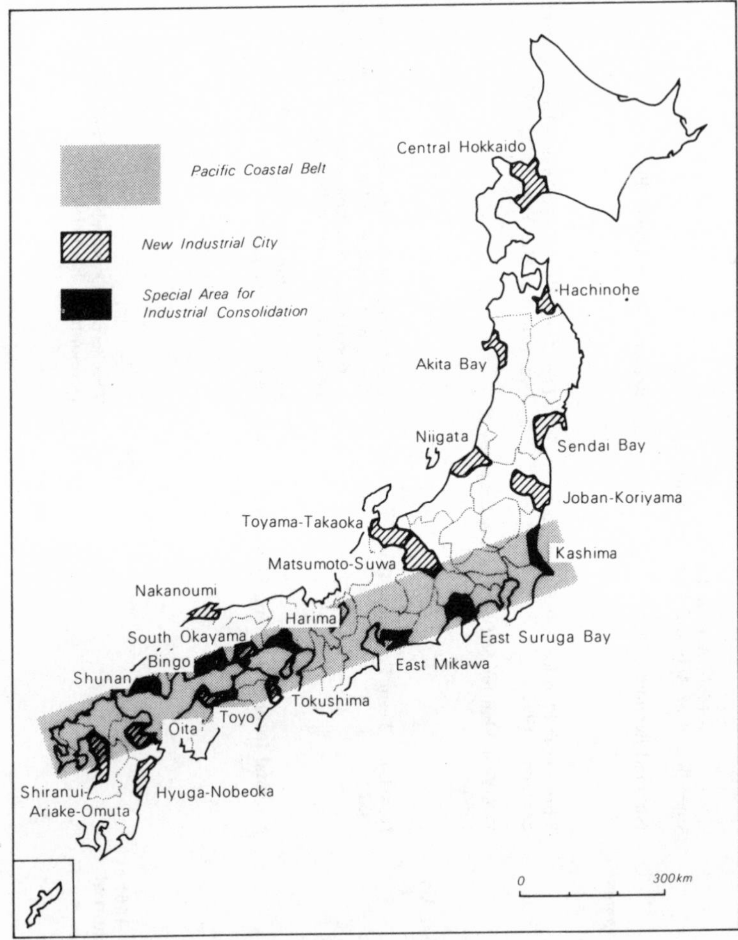

Fig. 6.1 Pacific coastal belt and designated areas

economic efficiency and handicap development.

The main point of the location policy in the Doubling Plan was to emphasise infrastructure improvement in the areas most advantageous for rapid development of industries, and to attract enterprises to these areas. In fact the Pacific Coastal Belt, comprising four major industrial areas, was planned to account for 87% of the industrial shipments of the whole country in 1970.

TABLE 30

The Main Acts and Plans
(Amendments of Acts and Plans are omitted)

Main Acts	National Economic Plans	Regional Development Plans
The Comprehensive National Development Act, 1950		
Hokkaido Development Act, 1950		
	Three Year Plan for Self-Supporting Economy, 1951	The Comprehensive Hokkaido Development Plan (the first Five Year Plan), 1951
	Five Year Plan for Self-Supporting Economy, 1955	
National Capital Region Development Act, 1956		
Tohoku Development Act, 1957	New Long Term Economic Plan, 1957	The Comprehensive Hokkaido Development Plan (the Second Five Year Plan), 1957
		National Capital Region Master Plan, 1958
		Tohoku Development Plan, 1958
Kyushu Development Act, 1959		Kyushu Development Plan, 1959
Shikoku Development Act. 1960	National Income Doubling Plan, 1960	Shikoku Development Plan, 1960
Hokuriku Development Act, 1960		
Chugoku Development Act, 1960		
Act for the Industrial Development in Underdeveloped Areas, 1961		
Act for Development of Water Resources, 1961		
Coal Mining Area Development Act, 1961		
Act for the Development of New Industrial Cities, 1962		The Second Comprehensive Hokkaido Development Plan, 1962

		The Comprehensive National Development Plan, 1962
Kinki Region Development Act, 1963		Hokuriku Development Plan, 1964
Act for the Development of the Special Areas for Industrial Consolidation, 1964		Hokuriku Development Plan, 1964
		Chugoku Development Plan, 1964
Rural Areas Development Act, 1965	Middle Term Economic Plan, 1965	Kinki Region Master Plan, 1965
Chubu Region Development Act, 1966		
	Economic and Social Development Plan, 1967	
		New Comprehensive National Development Plan, 1969
Under-Developed Area Development Act, 1970	New Economic and Social Development Plan, 1970	The Third Comprehensive Hokkaido Development Plan, 1970
Act for Promotion of Industrialisation in Farm Areas, 1971		
Industrial Relocation Promotion Act, 1972		Okinawa Development Plan, 1972

THE COMPREHENSIVE NATIONAL DEVELOPMENT PLAN

The National Income Doubling Plan as a national economic plan outlined the conception of the Pacific Coastal Belt; the details of the regional plan were committed to the Comprehensive National Development Plan, 1962 (1962 Plan). The National Income Doubling Plan as published was strongly criticised for focussing on efficiency and therefore giving priority to advanced areas. The 1962 Plan accordingly amended in part the policy of the National Income Doubling Plan and introduced the concept of 'preventing excessive expansion of urban areas and correcting regional imbalance'. In carrying out the regional policy of the 1962 Plan the following three categories of areas were designated by independent Acts respectively:

THE NEW INDUSTRIAL CITY

The New Industrial City was conceived as an area for centralised industrial development, with 1,000 ha of industrial land and 300 ha of housing land. Fifteen areas were designated, the minimum conditions being that the area was such as would be able to increase the population by 200,000 persons and the industrial shipments by 3,000 hundred million yen by the target year. In order to promote dispersal of industries and correct regional imbalance, designation in remote areas was emphasised, but at the same time, because of the current trend of industrial development, priority in designation was given to coastal areas suitable for location of heavy and chemical industries.

THE SPECIAL AREA FOR INDUSTRIAL CONSOLIDATION

While selection of the New Industrial City gave some priority to under-developed areas in order to reduce regional imbalance, the Special Areas for Industrial Consolidation were designated along the Pacific Coastal Belt. Investment efficiency, already high, made this the best part of Japan for promoting economic growth along with the industrial development of Japan. The scale of each designated area was twice that of New Industrial Cities.

THE AREA FOR INDUSTRIAL DEVELOPMENT OF AN UNDERDEVELOPED REGION

The area for Industrial Development of an Underdeveloped Region aimed at increasing the employment and lifting the economic standard of the area by industrial development. Inducements for factories to be located in the designated area included special depreciation allowances and exemption from rates (80% of exempted rates being filled by the Government). One hundred and five Areas for Industrial Development of an Underdeveloped Region were designated during the period 1962–6, but thereafter those which had reached a certain standard were released and the number decreased to 93 in 1973.

THE NEW COMPREHENSIVE NATIONAL DEVELOPMENT PLAN

In the later 1960s it became clear the industrial location plan of the Comprehensive National Development plan would be realised well before the target year, and at the same time serious environmental issues arose out of the rapid industrial development. Particularly in inner Tokyo, agglomeration of central management functions intensified and in the peripheral areas industrial agglomeration pushed outwards, which increased the evil effect of overcrowding and over-enlargement. In these circumstances positive dispersal of industry and population by advancing large scale development in remote areas was attempted, while high growth was still maintained, and it was to aid this development that the New Comprehensive National Development Plan (1969 Plan) was established. In this plan, concepts such as the network of SHINKANSEN (super express railway)[1] and highway, industrial development, environmental conservation and broad living sphere were embodied, but the Industrial Development Plan was drafted separately. This plan visualised an areal distribution of shipment by value, as shown in Table 30, on the

[1] SHINKANSEN is a super-express railway which started operation in October 1964 to connect Tokyo and Osaka and has been extended to Hakata in Northern Kyushu. The maximum speed is 210 km and the average speed 170 km per hour. It covers the distance between Tokyo and Osaka (533 km) in 3 hours 10 minutes and the distance between Tokyo and Hakata (1177 km) in 6 hours 56 minutes.

assumption that industrial shipments by value in 1985 would be 5.4 times the 1965 values, or, 160 billion yen. It planned to reduce the growth rates in Kanto and Kinki and to reduce their regional shares correspondingly. The land area required for the new industrial development is 200 thousand ha, one half of it in remote coastal areas, which include East Tomakomai (Hokkaido), Mutsu-Ogawara (North East Tohoku), Central Ise (Ise Bay), West Seto Inland Sea, Shibushi (Southern Kyushu), and the remaining half in inland areas. Control by law was considered necessary to promote dispersal to remote areas by suppressing location in the peripheral areas of large cities. The resulting Industrial Relocation Promotion Act, 1972, incorporates two major concepts: Departure Promotion Areas for regions already overcrowded and over-enlarged, which should expel some industries, and Relocation Reception Areas for regions which should attract new industries. Departure Promotion Areas are the existing urban areas of The National Capital Sphere and Kinki region, and the built-up area of Nagoya City. Relocation Areas cover 86.5% of national land. Inducements such as loans, subsidies and tax incentives are offered to industries moving to Relocation Reception Areas, and industrial parks are to be established by the Regional Development Corporation.

ACHIEVEMENTS OF POLICIES

The achievements of the New Industrial Cities and Special Areas for Industrial Consolidation are shown in Table 32. The result must be considered a success, since more than 13% real average annual growth was achieved, despite the fact that chronic depression persisted after the oil panic of 1973, and a real achievement ratio of 93% in the total average was realised a year before the target year. The population also increased from 14,180,000 in 1965 to 16,360,000 in 1975, accompanying the development of industry.

Public investment was 6.8 billion yen, with the share of investment for the production base larger than that for inhabitants' life, 55% in the New Industrial Cities and 63% in the Special Areas for Industrial Consolidation. Moreover, as Fig. 6.2 shows, the target achievement ratio of investment for the production base is higher. So city planning performance

TABLE 31

Regional Share of Industrial Shipments (percentage by value)

	Achievement in 1965	Target 1975	1985
Hokkaido	2.6	2.6	3.0
Tohoku	4.6	5.5	6.8
Kanto	35.5	35.0	32.7
Tokai	16.3	17.6	19.0
Hokuriku	2.3	2.4	2.4
Kinki	23.5	20.1	18.0
Chugoku	7.1	8.1	8.2
Shikoku	2.5	2.7	2.7
Kyushu	5.7	6.0	7.3
JAPAN	100.0	100.0	100.0

Source: MITI, Reference Data for Industrial Relocation Plan, 1977

lagged in these areas, resulting in environmental damage which could have been avoided.

Originally the 1962 Plan policy was to place emphasis on remote areas by correcting the priority given to the Pacific Coastal Belt. The New Industrial City was designed as a means for realising the 1962 Plan, its purpose being to reduce the regional imbalance in industry, population and income

TABLE 32

Target and Achievements of New Industrial Cities and Special Areas for Industrial Consolidation (Shipments by Value, hundred mil. yen)

	Target in 1975	Achievement 1965	Achievement 1974	Real Achievement Ratio for Target*	Real Annual Average Growth Ratio 1965–74*
New Industrial Cities	77,670	23,888	123,251	93	13.1
Special Areas for Industrial Consolidation	63,940	17,780	94,863	90	13.6
Total	141,610	41,668	218,114	90	13.6

Source: National Land Agency, Current State of New Industrial Cities and Special Areas for Industrial Consolidation, 1977.

*The figures of Achievement are nominal, but Achievement Ratio and Growth Ratio have been deflated to the prices of 1965.

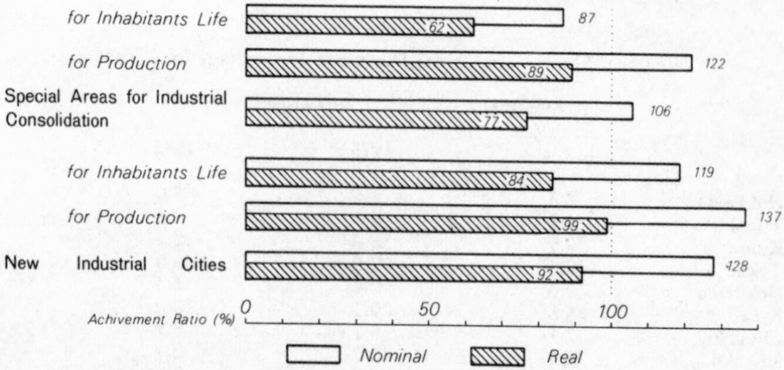

Fig. 6.2 Achievements of investments providing infrastructure. 1974 Fiscal Year %

through New Industrial Cities. Since, however, the Special Area for Industrial Consolidation was designated concentrally in the Pacific Coastal Belt as a means for maintaining high growth, one half of the designated New Industrial Cities and Areas for Industrial Consolidation were located in the Pacific Coastal Belt (Fig. 6.1). Further, 65% of the total industrial shipment value target is concentrated in the Pacific Coastal Belt.

As mentioned above, the industrial location policy, which was intended for dispersal, resulted in concentration, and the regional share of the Pacific Coastal Belt, which connects

TABLE 33

Change of Regional Share: Percentage by Value of Shipments of Manufactured Goods

	Target for 1975	Achievement 1965	Achievement 1975
Hokkaido	2.6	2.6	2.5
Tohoku	5.5	4.6	5.5
Kanto	35.0	35.5	34.7
Tokai	17.6	16.2	16.9
Hokuriku	2.4	2.3	2.4
Kinki	20.1	23.5	20.7
Chugoku	8.1	7.1	8.3
Shikoku	2.7	2.4	2.9
Kyushu	6.0	5.8	6.2
JAPAN	100.0	100.0	100.0

Source: MITI, Reference Data for Industrial Relocation Plan, 1977

existing main industrial regions, indicates almost no reduction. On the other hand, in the three major urban spheres of Tokyo, Osaka and Nagoya, which were designated as departure promotion areas under the Industrial Relocation Promotion Act, industrial land was reduced by approximately 1,400 ha between 1973 and 1975. This reflected the negative effect arising from overcrowding and over-enlargement and the positive effect of the incentive of the policy, while in relocation reception areas 84,000 ha of industrial land was obtained by enterprises during the same period and partial or full operation has begun. In the result, as Table 33 shows, the share of the Kanto and Kinki regions somewhat decreased and the share of other regions increased.

NEW POLICIES

As Table 33 shows, the effect of the Industrial Relocation Promotion Act, the reduction of the share of existing regions and the increase of dispersal to remote areas are witnessed by the figures. However, the share of the three major regions and the Pacific Coastal Belt was still large, and, therefore, policies for reducing the regional imbalance of industry, population and income by preventing outflow of population from less populated regions needed accentuated action.

Table 32 shows that the New Industrial Cities and the Special Areas for Consolidation attained 93% of the target in 1974, but the spread effect and the increase of population were less than the expectation of the plan. The Government, therefore, decided to extend the period of the plan for five years in these designated regions. The industrial shipment value target was raised from 21.8 billion yen in 1974 to 35.5 billion yen in 1980, and it is expected that the ratio of the industrial shipment value against the entire country will grow from 17% in 1974 to 19.3% in 1980 and that employment will increase by 920,000. On the other hand, drastic amendment of the 1969 Plan having become necessary through stagnation of industrial development in the chronic depression following the oil panic, the Third Comprehensive National Development Plan (November 1977) was drawn up. This Plan reduced the expected growth rate to 6% per year to correspond to the current low economic growth. Industrial production is estimated at 245 billion yen for 1985 and 310 billion yen for 1990, against 127.5 billion yen in 1975, and it is intended to tighten the control over the Tokyo and Osaka regions and to emphasise dispersal to remote areas.

2

Industrial Development and Environmental Issues

K. MURATA

Environmental pollution by industrial activity is not a new problem, but has accompanied the development of modern industry. Air pollution, water pollution, noise and vibration had already occurred in newly developed industrial cities in Japan in the 1890s. After 1920 water discharge from chemical industries caused damage to fishing in the coastal areas of Tokyo Bay, and after 1930 ground subsidence following excessive pumping of underground water occurred in major industrial cities. It was after 1960, however, when industrial production expanded extremely rapidly, that environmental problems became really serious.

Since the national land of Japan is mountainous, the area available for utilisation is only 70,000 km^2, 18% of the national land area, and the GNP per unit of area is 12 times as much as that of the USA, 3.2 times as much as that of the UK, and twice as much as that of Germany in 1970. Thus, the spatial density of production in Japan is much higher than in other industrialised countries, and, moreover, as mentioned in preceding chapters, since manufacturing industry is centralised in a small number of areas, environmental pollution is also concentrated in a small number of areas. For example, 76% sulphur oxides and 68% BOD load are localised in the Pacific Coastal Belt. As we have seen, the Pacific Coastal Belt is where the industrial location policy of the Government was centrally directed. Accordingly, the industrial location policy heightened the efficiency of industrial production and promoted economic development, but at the same time this centralisation intensified environmental pollution. Consequently, the Government reinforced countermeasures during the 1960s and enterprises also made preventive efforts, and the situation is gradually improving.

THE CURRENT STATE OF ENVIRONMENTAL POLLUTION AND DAMAGE

The situation with air pollution varies considerably, depending on the pollutants. Sulphur oxides, after reaching a peak concentration during 1965–8, show a downward trend. Coming in the last few years, at a time when the volume of petroleum-derived fuel consumption has increased, this may be claimed to indicate the effectiveness of such measures as the establishment of emission standards, increased imports of low-sulphur crude and heavy oil and industrial efforts toward desulphurisation among others. The presence of suspended particles, too, has been less evident since 1969, in spite of the potential for increase accompanying economic expansion. This may be attributed particularly to installation of control equipment (e.g. electric dust collectors) in pollutant-generating sources, to improved performance and to a reduction in the use of coal-related fuels. Carbon monoxide, too, after reaching a peak around 1969, is showing signs of decrease in Tokyo and Osaka. At the same time, it is becoming rarer to find cases of non-compliance with environmental standards.

Water pollution, too, is being gradually alleviated after a peak in 1971, but many areas have still not reached the environmental quality standard. Water quality pollution by organic matter derives not only from factory drains but also from domestic drains or the hot-water drains of generating plants. In manufacturing industry, the pollution load of pulp and paper manufacturing and other chemical industries is the highest. In sea areas, Tokyo Bay, Osaka Bay, Seto Inland Sea and others are heavily polluted. The COD that flows into Tokyo Bay averages 700-800 tons per day and in spring and summer reaches 8–15 ppm. The pollution of Ise Bay and the Seto Inland Seas was caused by the industries and urbanisation that rapidly expanded after the war, and COD is 2–5 ppm in both Ise Bay and Seto Inland Sea. Although a tendency to improvement is seen in these marine areas, generation of red tides is increasing, particularly in the Seto Inland Sea, where 300 cases were recorded in 1975 and 326 in 1976, causing serious damage to fishing.

Ground subsidence has occurred in 41 districts of the

country. Over the past 50 years, ground subsidence in the Koto district of Tokyo was approximately 4 metres and in the Konohana district of Osaka, 3 metres, the major cause being pumping up of underground water for industrial use. Even now 45% of industrial water in Japan is underground water, but since 1955, pumping up of underground water has been restricted in major industrial areas, which now draw their water from industrial water supply systems, and ground subsidence, once conspicuous in industrial cities such as Osaka, Kawasaki, Amagasaki, has almost stopped.

POLLUTION DAMAGE

A most serious problem of pollution damage is the damage to human health. Where a person's health is affected by atmospheric pollution or water quality pollution he is officially recognised as a 'victim of pollution' under the law for Relief of Damage to Health, 1973, and in 1976 there were 31,961 officially recognised victims of air pollution and 1,450 recognised victims of water pollution. Air pollution causes respiratory diseases, and most of the patients are residents in the three major industrial regions. A typical disease from water pollution is Minamata disease. Minimata disease in the Shiranui Coastal Area on the west coast of Middle Kyushu is an impairment of the central nervous system caused by poisoning through intake over a long period of large quantities of contaminated fish and shellfish caught in the Minamata Bay. Methyl mercury compounds produced in the aceto-aldehyde and acetic acid manufacturing facilities of the Minamata plant of the Chisso Corporation were discharged into the bay along with factory waste water and were accumulated in the bodies of fish and shellfish. By eating such seafood in large quantities the residents of the area contracted the disease.

Minamata disease in the Agano River Basin of Niigata Prefecture is also an ailment of the central nervous system caused by alkyl mercury through the medium of river fish. Here, too, the cause was organic mercury waste water, discharged by the Showa Denko Company. The recognised Minamata disease patients from 1955, when the disease was first recognised, up to 1976, reached 1,385 persons and deaths numbered 190 in 1976. The damage done by polluted water has spread to agriculture and fishing. In 1976, 165 thousand ha of agricultural land was subject to damage, 47% of which was from the waste water of industrial plants and the rest from contaminated water from mines and urban areas. The contamination of irrigation water not only does direct damage to agricultural products but also lowers the quality of the soil, which decreases productivity. For example, organic matter and nitrogen components are contained in the waste water discharged from pulp manufacturing plants and starch manufacturing plants in large quantities, and alkaline substances are contained in the waste water from chemical plants, mine areas and others, which cause various kinds of damage to the development of agricultural products. The effects of water pollution on the fishing industry include: (1) reducing operational efficiency and the catch; (2) deflated product prices or unsaleability, brought about by heavy metals and PCBs which have accumulated in the product; (3) deflated product prices or unsaleability brought about by offensive odours or deformity of the product; (4) increasing costs to restore polluted fishing grounds. Pollution in 1975 caused damage in 443 cases, estimated at 40 hundred million yen, and in a further 211 cases the value of damage was unknown. Most of the damage was done by oil and red tide, and in 16 sea areas polluted by mercury and PCB fishing is controlled.

The loss from ground subsidence generates large, but unquantifiable social costs. Submersion and destruction of houses and death and injury of human lives in large numbers from high tides occurred in coastal areas where ground subsidence was great in the 1950s. As countermeasures in such ground subsidence areas pumping up of underground water was prohibited and a large scale tide embankment was constructed, but in many of the newly developed industrial areas ground subsidence is still going on because of pumping up of underground water, since water supply by industrial water supply systems is insufficient.

PROGRESS IN ENVIRONMENTAL ADMINISTRATION

In the later 1950s pollution of air and water became serious in the industrial areas newly developed after the war as well as in the established industrial regions. For example, diseases such as bronchial asthma and asthmatic bronchitis, were generated by sulphur oxide in Yokkaichi City, where a petro-chemical industrial complex was developed. The example of Yokkaichi City stimulated residents' movements against new industrial developments, and in Nishinomiya City and Mishima-Namazu district the location of an oil refinery, petro-chemical works and steam power generation plants was cancelled because of the strong opposition of the residents.

Given this situation, the government passed the Basic Law for Environmental Pollution, 1968. Firstly, this law clarifies the respective responsibilities for environmental pollution control of the enterprise by the State, local governments and citizens. Secondly, it provides for environmental standards relating to air pollution, water pollution and noise, and stipulates that policies for environmental pollution control must be implemented in an overall and effective manner to maintain these standards. Thirdly, it lays down what the national and local governments shall do with regard to environmental pollution control. At the same time, it requires environmental pollution control programmes to be formulated for specific areas. This law also includes provision for the establishment of systems to provide relief in cases of damage or harm related to environmental pollution, for the financing of environmental pollution control and the necessary fiscal measures, and for the establishment, as Government organs, of the Conference on Environmental Pollution Control and the Central Council on Environmental Pollution Control.

Since the enactment of the Basic Law for Environmental Pollution Control, and in accordance with the spirit of this law as well as that of the Air Pollution Control Law, the Water Quality Maintenance Law, the Factory Effluent Control Law, the Noise Regulation Law and others, the regulation of sources of environmental pollution has been strengthened. Moreover, various laws relating to environmental pollution were enacted, such as the Law for the Settlement of Environmental Pollution Disputes and the Special Law Concerning Relief for Patients related to Environmental Pollution. Environmental quality standards have been set for sulphur oxides, carbon monoxide and water pollution, while the Government has been encouraging the installation of environmental pollution control facilities, technological development and the use of low-sulphur fuels to achieve and maintain these standards.

In the meantime, however, pollution has become more and more complex, and air pollution caused by lead in automobile exhaust, soil pollution caused by cadmium and the hazards posed by industrial waste among others, have also begun to play a part. Faced with this situation, the Government embarked upon a comprehensive review of the legal system relating to environmental pollution control, including the Basic Law for Environmental Pollution Control. As a result of this review work, in the extraordinary session of the Diet held late in 1970, fourteen laws and amendments were passed, including amendments to the Basic Law for Environmental Pollution Control, in order to strengthen the legal basis for pollution control.

As is generally known, guiding principles concerning international aspects of environmental policy were adopted at a council meeting of the Organisation for Economic Cooperation and Development (OECD) in May 1972. They were primarily concerned with the distribution of pollution control costs in promoting rational use of environmental resources and with avoiding strain in international trade and investment. Following these principles, polluters should pay for their own pollution control costs, and subsidies which bring about strain in international trade and investment should not be provided by governments.

Though compensation for damage and restoration costs for destroyed environment are not included in these principles, legal control of the environment in Japan is stricter and does not include compensation for health and property. The fundamental thought supporting strict legal control is the concept of 'social costs'. This concept is necessary to supplement 'defect of market economy' and gives theoretical foundation to the fact that enterprises have to internalise the social costs they have previously externalised, or, in other words, to pay the costs for environmental pollution. Air pollution occurs by the enterprise's behaviour, which economises production costs based on the market mechanism. If enterprises introduce control techniques to the production process, they internalise social costs in advance; when, however, they compensate for the damage to health and property, they internalise the social costs only after the damage has been done.

Legal control for pollution based on a concept of social costs has become stringent lately. In order to maintain environmental quality standards, enterprises have to pay heavily in investment for pollution control. For instance, the average pollution control investment of all manufacturing industries was 13% of the total equipment investment in 1965, but gradual increase thereafter raised it to 17.1% in 1975 (Table 34).

TABLE 34

Ratio of Pollution Control Investments to Equipment Investments, 1975

All Industries	17.1
Iron and Steel	17.9
Petroleum refinery	34.4
Steam power generation	47.4
Pulp and paper	24.6
Chemicals	32.0
Machinery	5.0
Cement	15.1
Petro-chemical	22.3

Source: Ministry of International Trade and Industry, 1975

These efforts of enterprises were made to meet the prescribed environmental quality standards, based on the Basic Law, in individual areas. Furthermore, the Environmental Agency obliged 50 areas to formulate pollution control programmes, according to which individual areas must attain their targets during the period of 1977–80. Local Governments are given powers to set emission standards for enterprises for attaining the target and to perform on-the-spot inspection and issue improvement orders. Eighty per cent of the major regions of the country have attained the environmental quality standard as a result of efforts made by the central and local governments and the enterprises themselves, and for BOD or COD 60% of 1426 areas including rivers, lakes and sea areas have attained the standard. Location of new plant is controlled by the Location of Industry Act, 1973, in addition to the Basic

Law. This law prescribes the ratios of production facilities, environmental facilities, green spaces, etc., of industrial land to be adhered to where a plant is newly established or enlarged. For instance, the building-to-land ratio for a petroleum refinery is limited to 10%, for pulp and paper, iron and chemicals to 20% and for the majority of other industries to 30%, and all kinds of industry must keep more than 20% in green space. Furthermore, environmental impact assessment is carried out where a large scale industrial development is planned, since its impact on the environment is great, and the Environment Agency may impose alteration and/or reduction of the plan, depending upon the assessment.

A most important aspect of the environmental administration is the relief system of damage to health. Prefectural governors 'recognise' health victims of pollution, and recognised patients are given medical costs and child allowances. If a patient dies, family compensation, funeral costs and other expenses are paid. The funds required for this relief are paid by industry – on the principle that the polluters pay.

Index

Compiled by Denis J. Nisbet